KABBALAH

A Gift

OF

The Bible

ACKNOWLEDGEMENTS

Our greatest debt is to Dr. Samuel R. Anteby for bringing *A Gift Of The Bible* from the original Hebrew out into the English speaking world. We are extremely grateful to Dr. Anteby, whose ideas and editorial assistance have been invaluable in his translation of this.

We are also most grateful to Holly Clark for secretarial help.

Research Centre Book of Related Interest
Ask your bookseller for the books you have missed

ENTRANCE TO THE ZOHAR, compiled and edited by Dr. Philip S. Berg
ENTRANCE TO THE TREE OF LIFE, compiled and edited by Dr. Philip S. Berg
KABBALAH FOR THE LAYMAN, by Dr. Philip S. Berg
TEN LUMINOUS EMANATIONS, vol. 1, compiled and edited by R. Levi Krakovsky
TEN LUMINOUS EMANATIONS, vol. 2, compiled and edited by Dr. Philip S. Berg
LIGHT OF REDEMPTION, by R. Levi Krakovsky
GENERAL PRINCIPLES OF KABBALAH, by R.M. Luzatto
THE KABBALAH CONNECTION, by Dr. Philip S. Berg
REINCARNATION: THE WHEELS OF A SOUL, by Dr. Philip S. Berg

BOOKS IN PRINT

KABBALISTIC ASTROLOGY, by Dr. Philip S. Berg
POWER OF THE ALEPH BETH, by Dr. Philip S. Berg
KABBALISTIC MEDITATION, by Dr. Philip S. Berg

Rabbi Yehuda Ashlag

KABBALAH

A Gift

OF

The Bible

Research Centre of Kabbalah
Jerusalem — New York

ISBN: 0-943688-22-1

First Printing, July 1984

For further information address:
Research Centre of Kabbalah
P.O.Box 14168
The Old City, Jerusalem, Israel
or
The Research Centre of Kabbalah
200 Park Ave. Suite 303E
New York, N.Y. 10017

BRANCHES IN ISRAEL
Tel Aviv, Safed, Haifa, Beer Sheva, Tikvah Quarter, Neveh Zedek
Quarter, Rehovot, Herzlia, Ashkelon

Printed in Israel 1984

PART ONE
THE MYSTICAL REVELATION

Chapter 2. The Giving of The Torah 30

PART TWO
THE ROOTS IN KABBALAH

Chapter 10. This Is For Yehuda 146

Chapter 11. Unification 151

FOREWORD

There is no end to the spiritual frontier. You can venture into life with a purpose.

People are living longer these days, yet they find living difficult. Government concern with our problems and rising standard of living has not enhanced the feeling of human worth. On the contrary, most people have retreated from life into a negative pattern of living. The arch enemy of creative living is the pessimistic patterns people are falling into. We are telling ourselves that we are meaningless numbers in a vast world. We pamper ourselves on a diet of entertainment. We have become watchers and observers in a world that is passing us by.

It is therefore a great pleasure to write a foreword to this volume. Even a glance at the table of contents will indicate the range covered by Rabbi Ashlag's examination of the inter-relation and interaction between the spiritual and physical realm, particularly:

1) their impact upon the crisis of modern life;
2) the effects of "love thy neighbor";
3) the giving of the Bible; and
4) the relationship between the Jew and non-Jew in the Messianic era.

I am confident this book will provide the reader with new hope. Too much negative thinking is eating away at people's minds these days. There is simply to many people wasting away their lives feeling depressed, asking what is life all about.

It is only realistic to say that, in this "age of Aquarius", your life and years ahead can be happy and fulfilling ones.

Dr. Philip S. Berg

A NOTE TO THE READER

This book is a collection of three booklets, "The Giving of Torah", "Mutual Responsibility" and "Peace" which appeared in the year 5693 (1973) from Rabbi Yehuda Ashlag.

Fifty such booklets were originally supposed to appear but due, to various reasons at the time, only the first three appeared.

In this edition, we have added two articles entitled "Freedom of Choice" and "Individual Freedom" which were to have constituted a portion of the fourth booklet.

We have similarly included "An Article On the Completion of the Zohar" which was said when printing of the "Sulam" commentary on the Zohar by the author was completed. The speech was given at a dinner given in Miron on the 23rd day of the *Omer* in 5713 (1953).

At the end of the book we have also added an article "And this is for Judah", from the explanation of the Passover Haggadah which was printed in 5690 (1930) and an article on "Unity" from the author's manuscripts.

INTRODUCTION

It Is Time To Act

For some time now, I have felt a daily need to do something out of character and write a basic article on the soul of Judaism and a knowledge of the origins of Kabbalistic Wisdom. I wish to make it available to the general public in a manner that they will glean from it a recognition and understanding of the category of things which stand at the heights of the world in a proper way according to their true character and nature. Traditionally in Judaism, prior to the introduction of the printing press, there were in our midst no fraudulent books on topics touching on the soul of Judaism. We had in our midst no authors who were not responsible for their words.

The reason for this was simple. An irresponsible person is usually not among the most famous. If perchance such a person had the nerve to write a composition such as this, no scribe would find it worthwhile to copy his book. His efforts would not be rewarded, for they (his efforts) would be enormous. Such a book would therefore be lost to the public.

In this time period, even those who knew their subject matter had no cause to write a book such as this one. Knowledge of these areas is not critical to the public at large. On the contrary, they had reason to hide these subjects in hidden places because "hiding things is respectful to G-d". We Jews have been commanded to hide the soul of the Torah and service from those who have no need for it or are unworthy of it. We should not degrade and publicly display it to satisfy the desires of those who peep through windows or those who seek thrills. Our respect for G-d demands this of us.

However, once the printing press spread worldwide and authors no longer relied on copyists, the high cost of books went down. Along with this, the way was prepared for irresponsible authors to write books as they desired for profit, respect, etc. The contents of what they write is not taken into consideration and they don't look at all at the works they have created.

From that time on, the number of books described above began to increase. Without any direct learning of Kabbalah from a qualified teacher, and even without any knowledge of the early books on the subject, the authors went ahead and brought opinions from their own minds and from every absurdity imaginable. They raised their ideas to the very heavens and thereby painted the great treasure of the jewish nation. Like fools, they had no knowledge of the proper precautions to take. Instead they brought mixed-up ideas to future generations. And in exchange for their miniscule desires, they sinned and caused future generations to do likewise.

Finally, their stench rose higher and higher. For they have sunk their fingernails into the Kabbalistic wisdom without considering the fact that this wisdom is enclosed within a thousand rings, so that today, those who delve into it are unable to understand even a single word. That is to say nothing of the connection between one word and the next. For all the true books hitherto published contain only the finest of hints. They scarcely suffice an erudite student with a Kabbalistic sage and even then he has difficulty in understanding the explanations of their passages.

And now "the rattlesnakes have made their nest there, laid and hatched (their eggs), and brood under her shadow". (Isaiah, 34:15). In our day, these sorcerers* (a play on words on authors) have increased in number. They make tidbits like these which are revolting to all who look at them. There are even those who have soared to the Zenith and appropriated for themselves the position reserved for the greats of each generation. They make themselves into people who know how to explain the early works, then tell the public which books are worthy of study and which are unworthy and filled with dream and disillusion (G-d forbid!).

It is enough to raise contempt and anger. For until now, the job of explanation has traditionally been relegated to only one of the ten greats of each generation, and now the ignorant abuse it.

Therefore, public knowledge and grasp of these ideas has been confounded. In addition, an atmosphere of irresponsibility has been created. Everyone thinks that a single excursion to delve into and consider these lofty issues during a free hour is sufficient. They cover the entire world of this grand wisdom and the soul of Judaism in a single flight like an angel. Each reaches conclusions according to his own spirit.

These are the reasons which have taken me out of my usual character and why I have decided that it is time to act for the sake of G-d and save that which can still be saved. I have accepted upon my self to reveal a certain measure of the wisdom described above and to publicly spread it.

PART ONE

THE MYSTICAL REVELATION

CHAPTER 1

REVEALING A HANDBREADTH AND CONCEALING TWO

When reputable people are about to reveal something deep, a common statement of theirs is "Behold I am revealing a handbreadth and concealing two." Early authorities were cautious not to utter even a single extraneous word. As our Sages told us (TB Megillah 18a; Introduction to Zohar with Sulam commentary, 18): "A word is worth one sela', silence is worth two". This means that if you have something valuable to say which is worth one sela' (a monetary unit), then silence is worth two. These words are directed at those who spew extraneous words unrelated to the issue at hand solely for the purpose of beautifying the language for the reader. This is anathema to our early authorities, as is well known to all who look at their works, and as I will show in the following articles.

We must, therefore, proceed to understand this suggestion which was so natural to them.

Three Types of Concealment of Wisdom

There are three categories of Torah secrets, each having its own reason to be hidden. They are (a) the unnecessary, (b) the impossible and (c) G-d's secrets for the worthy. There is no small detail of this wisdom which does not have some aspect of these three associated with it. I will explain them one at a time.

(a) The Unnecessary

This means that no one will receive any benefit from its revelation. It is understood that we are not here referring to a great loss but only to a clearing of the mind, to be cautious in those areas referred to as "so what" (i.e., uncritical areas), that is, in areas where it makes no difference if you do something, for nothing is lost in doing so.

One should know that the Sages think of the "so what" category as the most awesome of all destroyers. For (almost) all people who were or will be created in this world are in the category of "so what". They engage themselves and others in unnecessary areas. Therefore, the Sages would not accept any pupil until they got from him reassurance that he would not reveal anything that was not necessary.

(b) The Impossible

This means that because of the great spirituality and ephemeral quality of the idea, the language is unable to describe any of their properties. Therefore, any attempt to enclothe them with words will only deceive those who delve into them and lead them in vainful paths. This is a sin too great to bear.

To reveal any of these ideas, therefore, one must have special Heavenly permission. This is the secret section of concealment of wisdom. This permission needs further elaboration.

Heavenly Permission

This subject is explained in the book "Portal of Rabbi Simon Bar Yohai's Sayings", by R. Isaac Luria (*on the Parsha of *Mishpatim* (Exodus 21:1), in the Zohar page 100, beginning "R. Bar Yohai from how to conceal").

"You should know that the souls of the righteous have an aspect of an encircling light and an inner light (an explanation can be found in *Panim Me'irot* in the Portal of Surroundings, Chapter 48, page 233). Those with a portion of the surrounding light have the ability to speak of hidden things and secrets of the Torah by way of much hiding and concealment. They do so in a manner such that only the worthy will understand them. R. Simon Bar Yohai's soul came from the surrounding light. He therefore had the ability to enclothe ideas and expand on them in a manner that even were he to expound on them publicly, only the worthy would understand him. He was therefore given permission to write the Zohar. Permission was not given to his Rabbis (teachers) or to other early authorities who followed him though there were certainly some who knew more of this wisdom than he did. But the reason is that hey did not have the ability to enclothe the words as he did. This is the meaning of what is written "Bar Yohai knows how to conceal his path". We now understand the great concealment in the Zohar written by R. Simnon Bar Yohai. For not every mind can understand his words.

'The essence of these words is that issues in Kabbalah do not at all depend on the greatness or smallness of the individual Kabbalist. Rather, it is an issue of the light that shines upon an individual's soul. This light of the soul is the Heavenly "permission" to reveal the supernal wisdom'.

From this we learn that one who does not have this permission is forbidden to give explanations of Kabbalah. He does not know how to express these ephemeral ideas with appropriate words in a manner that those who delve into it will not be ensnared.

For this reason we have not found any organized Kabbalistic work prior to the Zohar of R. Simon Bar Yohai. All the Kabbalistic books which preceded him are not considered explanations of Kabbalah but only hints. They are not arranged such that one subject logically follows another. This is well known to Kabbalists.

According to what I have received from teachers and books, I wish to add that no author from the time of R. Simon Bar Yohai until the Ari was able to explain the Zohar and the *Tikkunim* as did the Ari. All the books which preceded him are only hints of Kabbalistic wisdom. This includes the books on R. Moses Cordovero (RaMaC).

The Ari himself is deserving of those things that were said about R. Simon Bar Yohai. The Ari's predecessors were not granted the Heavenly permission to reveal Kabbalistic explanations, but the Ari did have such permission. This is not a matter of greatness or smallness. For it may have been that some of his predecessors were on a higher level than he. But they were not given permission for this task. They therefore restrained themselves from writing the explanations appropriate to the Kabbalah but were content with works containing short unconnected hints.

For this reason, from the time that the Ari's books were revealed to the world, all those who engage in Kabbalistic wisdom lay down the books of the Rav Moses Cordovero and other sages and authorities who preceded the Ari. This is well known among Kabbalists. Their hearts and souls cleaved only to the writings of the Ari. The books thought of as the proper explanation of Kabbalistic wisdom were only the Zohar, the *Tikkunim,* and then the writings of the Ari.

(c) G-d's Secrets to the Worthy

The meaning is that the secrets of the Torah are explained only to those who fear His name and guard His respect with all their hearts and souls. They would never profane G-d's name. This is the third category of concealing wisdom.

This category is the most severe. Those who revealed this aspect of Kabbalah created many pitfalls. From them we have those who make vows and amulets, and those who engage in practical Kabbalah, unknowingly damaging their own souls. We also have those who engage in various occult activities revealed by unworthy students. While they derive from them a personal or communal benefit, the world at large has and continues to suffer from it.

You should know that the whole root and purpose of concealing Kabbalistic wisdom was, from its very beginning, for this third category. For this reason the Sages were very cautious in examining the students. The Talmud says (TB *Chagigah* 13a) "The head of the Jewish court is only told the heads of chapters (i.e. superficial ideas), and then only if his heart yearns for it," and "We do not expound on the working of creation with only two (students present) nor on the workings of the chariot with only one". There are other similar statements.

All of this fear is based on what we explained above. And for this reason, very few merited to learn this wisdom. Even those who fulfilled the requirement of seven examinations and investigations were sworn with strict and awesome vows not to reveal any of the three categories discussed above at all. (See also the introduction to Sefer Yetzirah by R. Moshe Butorel).

I have divided concealment of Kabbalistic wisdom into three categories. Do not be misled to think that Kabbalah itself is divided in these three categories. Rather, my intent is that each and every word and detail of this vast wisdom has branches in all aspects of the three categories. Every detail in Kabbalah is explained on all three levels. It is important to understand this.

We may now ask a question. If concealing Kabbalistic wisdom did indeed reach such great levels, then where were the thousands of books written on the subject taken from? The answer is that there is a difference between the first two categories and the third. The primary burden of concealment is laid on the third category, for reasons discussed above.

The first two categories do not have a fixed restriction upon them. For something in the "Not Necessary" category may at times go out of that category and become necessary for whatever reason. Similarly, the "Impossible" category may at times become possible for one of two reasons. Either the generation develops and can now understand or Heavenly permission is granted. The latter occurred to R. Simon Bar Yohai and the Ari, and to a certain measure also to their predecessors. For these reasons, the true books composed until now were revealed and made public.

This is the intention of the Sages who said "I revealed a handbreadth and concealed two." They meant that something occurred enabling them to reveal something new which their predecessors hadn't considered. The single handbreadth refers to the one category of the three discussed above which they reveal while leaving two concealed. This is their indication that something has occurred to them, and the reason for their revelation. It may mean that the unnecessary became necessary or that they were given special Heavenly permission. This is what they mean when they say, "I revealed a handbreadth."

Those who study these articles should know that I intend to publish them throughout the course of a single year. Each of them is new and is not brought directly or quoted precisely from any book which precedes me. Rather, I received it directly from the mouth of my teacher who was well qualified for this task. That is, he too received it orally from his teacher, etc.

I received them with all the conditions of concealing and guarding it. But, beause of the necessity as I described in the Introduction, the unnecessary has become necessary. I have therefore revealed a handbreadth with complete permission as I explained above. The other two handbreadths, however, I will continue to guard, as I was commanded.

CHAPTER 2

THE GIVING OF THE TORAH

"Thou Shalt Love Thy Friend As Thyself" (Leviticus, 19:18). Rabbi Akiba says, "This is an important principle in Torah". (Genesis Rabbah, p. 24).

1) This Rabbinical saying calls for an explanation. For the word principle connotes an assemblage of specifics which, collectively creates a principle. We find therefore, that when he says the commandment "Love Thy Friend As Thyself" is an important principle in the Torah, we must understand that the other 612 *mitzvot* in the Torah, with all their explanations, are no more or less than the sum of the specifics contained and conditioned in this one commandment, "Love Thy Friend As Thyself."

2) Even if we are able to find some way of explaining these words, then there is a second more outstanding saying. When a convert came to Hillel, he said, "Teach me the whole Torah while I am standing on one leg". Hillel replied, "That which is hateful to thee, do not do to your fellow man," (This is the translation of Love Thy Friend) "The rest is commentary, go out and learn."

We have before us a clear *Halakha.* (Jewish law). None of the 612 *mitzvot* or other principles of the Torah is more important than "Love Thy Friend As Thyself." They only come to explain and permit us to keep the commandment of loving another as it should be kept. For it specifically says 'The rest is its explanation, go out and learn." That is that the rest of the Torah is an explanation of this single commandment. For it is impossible to complete the *mitzvah* of Love Thy Friend As Thyself without them.

3) Before we delve into the depths of the subject, we must reflect on the commandment itself. We are commanded, "Love Thy Friend As Thyself". The words "As Thyself" tell us that you should love your friend in the exact measure that you love yourself and not in any way less. That means that I must constantly be on my guard and fulfill the needs of each and every person in the entire Jewish nation. I must do this no less than I am always careful to fulfill my own needs.

But this is entirely impossible. Very few people are able, in a day's work to fulfill even their own needs. How do you obligate them to work further and fill the requests of the entire nation?

It is impossible to think that the Torah is exaggerating. The Torah warns us not to add or detract from what it says, thereby telling us that the commandments are stated with great specificity.

4) As if this were not enough for you, I will tell you that the literal meaning of this *mitzvah* of loving another further obligates us to give precedence to others' needs over our own.

Tosafot (Talmudic commentary), quotes the Jerusalem Talmud *(Kiddushin* p. 28a) on the sentence "for it is good for him with you", speaking about a Hebrew slave. *Tosafot* says,

"Sometimes he has only one pillow. If he sleeps on it himself and doesn't give it to his slave, then he is not keeping "for it is good for him with you". And if he doesn't sleep on it and he doesn't give it to his slave, then this is the character of Sodom. He is therefore forced to give it to his slave and the master himself must sleep on the ground".

Here we must learn the same law regarding loving another, for here too, the Torah compares fulfilling another's needs with fulfilling our own, as in the example of the Hebrew slave where "it is good for him with you". According to this, if he should have only one chair and his friend has none, the Halakhic ruling is that if he should sit on it and not give it to his friend, then he is violating the positive commandment of "Love Thy Friend As Thyself". He is not fulfilling the needs of the friends to the degree that he fulfills his own. And if he doesn't sit on it nor does he give it to his friend, then this is wickedness of the Sodomite level. Rather, he is obligated to give it to his friend to sit on, and he must either sit on the ground or stand.

It is self explanatory that this ruling applies to all possessions he has which a friend does not. Now go and see if it is possible to keep this commandment.

5) From the outset we must understand why the Torah was given specifically to the Jewish nation and was not given equally to all mankind. Is there here an element of nationalism, G-d forbid? Certainy not. No person would say this.

Our sages already addressed this question. The Talmud says *(Avodah Zarah,* 2b) that G-d offered it to all the nations and they refused it. According to this, it is difficult to understand how we can be called the chosen people, as it is written, "G-d chose you". None of the other nations wanted it!

The events themselves are difficult. Can it be that G-d took his Torah in hand and negotiated with those wild nations Himself or via one of His prophets? Something like this has never been heard of, nor is it acceptable.

6) When, however, we understand the quality of the Torah and the commandments given to us, and what is requested of us to keep them to the degree that our Sages have shown us, and that it is the purpose of the great creation set before our eyes, then we will understand everything.

It is a primary principle that there is no worker who works without a goal in mind. There are no exceptions to this rule except for the lowlifes in the human race or infants. There can therefore never be any doubt that the Creator, whose supremacy cannot be fathomed, should do something, small or large, without a purpose. Our Sages have taught us that the world was created only for the purpose of keeping the Torah and the *mitzvot*. As the early authorities have explained it, the intention of the Creator, from the moment he created the world, was to make His G-dliness known to others. And this acknowledgement of His G-dliness reached the creatures through the measure of His pleasant influence which increases up to the needed amount. In this way, those who are low are raised when they truly recognize this. They become a chariot for His influence and cleave to Him until they reach their final completeness.

The Bible says, "The eye has not seen another G-d but you" (Isaiah 64:3). The Torah and Prophets were unable to say even a word concerning this difference due to all the greatness and splendor of this completeness. Our Sages hinted at this when they said (TB *Berakhot*, 34b) "All the prophets prophesied for the days of the Messiah. But as for the world to come 'the eye has not seen another G-d but you". This is well known to

Kabbalists. Now is not the time to expand on it.

This completeness is expressed in the words of the Torah, prophets and our Sages with only the simple word "cleaving" *(D'vekut).* Due to semantic change in this word through popular usage, it has practically lost all meaning. But if you will let your thoughts dwell on this word for a moment, you will be astonished at its wonderful loftiness. It will paint for you the G-dly picture and the graceful worthiness of the lowly creature, man. Then you will be able to evaluate the relationship of the one cleaving to the other. Then you will understand why we utilize this word as representing the purpose of this great creation.

What comes out of this is that the purpose of creation is that the lowly creatures can, by keeping the Torah and commandments, rise higher and higher, developing continually until they are able to cleave to their Creator.

7) The Sages of the Zohar asked questions concerning this. Why did He not create us from the outset with the necessary majesty to cleave to Him? Why did He have to impose upon us this burden and bother of creation, Torah and commandments? They answered that one who eats not of his own is ashamed to look at the face of his benefactor.

The meaning is that one who eats and benefits from the toil of the hands of his friends is afraid to look at his friend's face. For he becomes humiliated and as a result of this he loses his humanity.

But when it comes from His completeness, there can be no lack of any quality. He therefore left room for us to gain for ourselves the desired majesty through observance of the Torah and commandments.

These things are very deep. I have already explained them sufficiently in another place (*Panim Masbirot* on *Etz Chayim*, First Chapter and Talmud *Eser Sefirot,* An Internal Look, Section 1). Here I will explain them briefly so they will be understood by all.

8) This is similar to a rich man who called in a man from the street. He fed him, gave him water and gave him money and everything desirable daily. Each day, the gifts increased. Finally, the rich man asked him, "Tell me, have all your desires been filled?" The poor man answered, "Not all my requests have been filled. For it would be much better and sweeter for me if I had earned all this delightful property on my own as you did Then I would not be receiving it through your loving kindness". The rich man replied, "There is no living creature who can fulfill that request".

This is only natural. On the one hand, the poor man has great pleasures which increase proportionately to the presents he receives. On the other hand, it is hard for him to suffer the embarassment from all the increasing favors which the rich man continues to do for him.

It is a natural law that a recipient feels a kind of shame and impatience when he receives a free gift from one who gives it to him through pity and the goodness of his heart. From this we derive a general law. There is no one in the world who can completely fulfill the desires of his friend. In the end, he cannot give him the character of self-attainment. Only with that is the contentment complete as desired.

This inability applies only to those who were created; it does not apply to His supernal completeness. He arranged for us to discover our own majesty for ourselves through the weariness and hardship of engaging the Torah and commandments. Then all the pleasure and good which comes to us from Him, that is, everything included in cleaving to Him, is entirely earned by us. It comes to us through our own handiwork. We then feel that we are masters over it. There is no flavor of completeness without our making an effort to earn it, as we have here explained.

9) Based on this, it is worthwhile for us to examine the source of this natural law. From where did this blemish of modesty and impatience which we feel when we receive a gift from someone derive?

The answer is well known to natural scientists. The nature of every branch is similar to that of its root. Everything that benefits the root is also beneficial to the branch. The latter desires them and derives benefit from them. On the other hand, anything not customarily at the root is avoided by the branch and is detrimental to it. This law applies to all roots and branches without exception.

From this, we can understand the source of the pleasures and punishments which are fixed in our world. Because G-d is the root of all the creations He created, then everything included within Him which is directly drawn to us is sweetened and pleasant for us, for our nature is similar to G-d, our root.

Anything not customarily associated with Him, which we do not derive directly from Him except via the axis of creation itself, is contrary to our nature and difficult for us to endure.

For example, we love rest and hate motion so much that we will not move except to attain rest. This is so because our Root is not itself a moving one but a resting one. The concept of movement does not apply to Him at all, G-d forbid. Therefore, it is also against our nature and despicable to us.

In this manner, we very much love wisdom, might and richness for all these are contained within G-d who is our Root. And we hate their opposites such as stupidity, weakness and poverty, for they are not at all found in our Root. These make us feel repugnant and hateful and cause us unbearable pain.

10) This is what gives us the tainted taste of embarassment and impatience when we receive something from another as a gift. For in our Creator Himself, there is no concept of receiving a favor. From whom shall He receive it? Because the idea does not exist in our Root it is therefore repugnant and hateful to us, as we have stated.

Similar to Him, we feel pleasure and sweetness each time we impart to another. This is customary in our Root, for He imparts to all.

11) We can now look at the purpose of creation, that is, "cleaving" to His true countenance. The entire concept of majesty and cleaving is promised to us through our handiwork in Torah and the commandments. This is nothing more than the leaves imitating their root. All the sweetness and pleasure and everything lofty is something which naturally flows of itself as we explained earlier.

The idea of pleasure is nothing more than the creation imitating its creator. When they are equal in every action customarily found in their root, then we have pleasures. Every event that happens to us from things not found in our root becomes unbearable, a burden to the soul, and outright painful. This is expected from the concept we described. We conclude that our entire hope depends on the degree to which we cause our natures to imitate that of our root.

12) These are the words of our Sages (Genesis Rabbah, Chap. 44) when they ask, "What difference does it make to G-d if one slaughters from the throat or the back of the neck?" They answer that "the commandments are not given for any purpose other than to draw the creatures together." This drawing together results in purification of the physical body. This is the purpose derived from keeping the entire Torah and commandments.

Man is born a wild beast. When he exits from the bosom of creation (his mother's womb) he is in a state of lowness and filth. This refers to the great self love in his nature; all his actions are strongly self-centered. There is not even the tiniest spark (hint) of altruism. In this manner, he is at the greatest possible distance from his Root, (G-d) that is, at the opposite extreme. The Root is totally altruistic without any sparks of receiving at all. The child who was born is in a state of receiving for itself alone without any sparks of imparting to another at all. Its status is therefore understood as being at the lowest possible point of lowliness and filth found in our physical world.

As the child grows, he learns from his environment partial lessons of altruism. This certainly depends on the opportunities his environment provides for his development. At that time, they also begin to train him in keeping the Torah and *mitzvot* for personal reasons –– for reward in this world and the world to come. This is called "not for its own sake". It is impossible to train him in any other way. As he grows and gets older, they reveal to him how to engage in the *mitzvot* "for their own sake", that is, with the sole intent of acting for the satisfaction of his Creator. The Rambam (Maimonides) writes (Laws of

Repentance, chap. 10) that "It is not proper to reveal how to engage in Torah and *mitzvot* for their own sake to women and little children for they will be unable to carry it out. When they mature and acquire knowledge and wisdom, then we teach them how to do it 'for its own sake!' Similarly, our Sages have said TB (*Pesachim,* 50b) "By doing it not for its own sake, he comes to do it for its own sake".

All this is encompassed within the intent of doing it for our Creator's satisfaction and not for any self-love, such as it may be. According to the natural virtue of engaging in Torah and *mitzvot,* mankind develops and goes to the higher leavels of majesty, spoken of. Finally, he is able to dissolve himself of all sparks of self-love and all the parts of his body are elevated. All of his actions are performed in a manner to impart to others. Even the necessities of life that he receives stream to him with the purpose of enabling him to impart to others.

The Giver of the Torah was aware of this, as our Sages have said (TB *Kiddushin,* 30a) "The L-rd said, 'I created the instinct to do evil. I created the Torah as an antidote for it'".

This is the meaning of the Sages' statement that "the commandments were given for the purpose of bringing human beings together".

13) There are two kinds of commandments in the Torah: (1) Those between man and G-d and (2) Those between man and his fellow man. Both of them have the same intent of bringing man to his final purpose of cleaving to G-d as we have explained. Not only this, but even the practical side of each have the same purpose. For when a person performs his actions for their own sake, without any admixture of self-love, that is, without deriving from it any personal benefit whatsoever, then

the person will not feel alienated from his own actions. This is true regardless of whether he does it out of love for his fellow man or his love for G-d.

Every action that a person performs for love of another is done with the help of a returning light, and a reward which in the end will return to help and serve his own purposes. These actions, therefore, cannot truly be called loving another when they are judged based upon their consequences. It can be compared to a salary that is not paid until completion of the act! In any case, an action performed for a salary cannot be considered loving another.

To perform an action totally for the purpose of loving another, that is without an aspect of a returning light and some hope of a reward which will ensue to him, is totally impossible according to natural law.

On this subject the Zohar says of the Gentile nations, "every good deed that they do is done for themselves". This means that all acts of kindness they do for their friends or in worshipping their gods is not done for love of another but for self-love. That is because this acting out of love for another goes contrary to nature, as we explained.

Therefore, only those who keep the Torah and commandments are capable of this. For when a person accustoms himself to keeping the Torah and *mitzvot* for G-d's satisfaction, then he is slowly able to leave the bosom of Nature and acquire a second nature, that of loving another, as we have said.

This is what made the Sages of the Zohar completely exclude the gentiles from the realm of loving one another. They said that "every good deed which they do is done for themselves", for they do not engage in the Torah for its own sake. All service that they do to their gods is for reward and salvation in this world and in the world to come. It turns out that the worship of their gods is also because of self-love. In any case, they can never have any action outside the realm of their own bodies. They cannot be raised even the smallest amount above the natural levels.

14) We see with our own two eyes that one who engages in the Torah and *mitzvot* for its own sake, feels no difference between the two divisions (between man and his fellow man; between man and G-d in the Torah. This is true even of the commandments requiring us to perform actions.

Before a person can be complete, it is mandatory that he think of every action he does for another, whether for G-d or for another person, as vain from every aspect. But, through his great labor, he is slowly raised and elevated to a second nature, as we have said before. Then he immediatley merits the final reward of cleaving to Him.

Since this is the case, it is reasonable that man can more easily attain the desired purpose with that portion of Torah having to do between man and his fellow man. Performance of *mitzvot* between man and G-d is fixed and no one makes demands. A person easily habituates himself in worship, and nothing done out of habit can, as is known, be of any value. This is not the case with commandments between man and his fellow man. They are not fixed and specific. Demands surround him wherever he turns. Therefore, their characteristics are more certain and their goal easier to attain.

15) We can now easily understand the words of Hillel the Prince to the convert. He said that the central axis of the Torah is "Love Thy Friend As Thyself". The rest of the 612

commandments between man and G-d are in the category of preparation for this commandment, it being the final purpose of emanating from the Torah and commandments. On this our Sages have said, "the Torah and *mitzvot* were given for the sole purpose of uniting Israel", as we said above in paragraphg 12. The reference is to purifying the body until one acquires a second nature of loving another. This single commandment of "Love Thy Friend As Thyself" is the final purpose of the Torah. After observing it, one immediately merits cleaving to G-d.

One should not ask why Hillel did not specify this with the statement "Thou shalt love the L-rd thy G-d with all they heart, and all thy soul and all that you have". This is so because of the reason we explained above. In truth, with respect to a man who is still within the nature of creation (i.e. still bound by natural laws) there is no difference between loving G-d and loving his friend. Everything external to himself is in the categorty of non-existent. The convert requested that Hillel explain to him the principles that the Torah desires of him in a way that his purpose shall "be near to him and not a distance away". He said, "Teach me the entire Torah while I am standing on one leg".

Hillel therefore explained it in terms of loving his friend because its purpose is closer and more quickly revealed (as discussed in paragraph 14). It is more guarded from mistakes and there are those who will make demands.

16) With what we have said we can understand the apparent contradiction we stated before (par. 3,4) concerning the essential contents of the commandment "Love Thy Friend As Thyself". How can the Torah obligate us to fulfill something

which is impossible?

Therefore, be enlightened! It is for this reason that the Torah was not given to our forefathers Abraham, Isaac and Jacob, but was instead delayed until the exodus from Egypt. At that time they left and became a complete nation of six hundred thousand men aged 20 years and older. At the Exodus, each and every one was asked if he agrees to this lofty service. And after each and every one agreed with one heart and one soul, and said, "We will do and we will hear", observing the principles of the Torah became possible. It went out of the cateogry of impossible and came into the category of possible.

This is a virtual certainty. Six hundred thousand men free themselves of all their actions for personal needs and they do nothing in their lives except to constantly stand guard that their friend should not lack anything.

In addition, they engage in this with great love with all their heart and soul as laid out in "Love Thy Friend As Thyself". Then it is certain that no individual need concern himself about his own sustenance. He thus becomes completely free of concern for his own sustenance and he can easily fulfill the commandment of "Love Thy Friend As Thyself" as explained in pars. 3 and 4. How could he fear for even a moment about his own sustenance? There are six hundred thousand loving, true men standing guard with a careful watch that he should lack none of his needs.

Therefore, after every member of the nation had agreed to it, the Torah was immediately given. For now they were capable of fulfilling it.

Prior to the time when they became a complete nation, not to mention at the time of the forefathers who were only individuals, they were incapable of keeping the Torah in the desired manner. In a small population it is impossible to even begin engaging in the commandments between man and his fellow man, centered around Love Thy Friend As Thyself. Therefore, the Torah was not given to our forefathers.

17) With what we have stated, we can understand one of the more surprising of our Sages' statements. They say that all of Israel are "responsible for one another".

At first glance, its purpose appears unjustified. For how can it be that one will sin or commit an iniquity and anger his Creator, and though I don't know him or have any relationship to him, G-d will exact his due from me. The Torah says, "Fathers shall not die (for the sins of their sons, nor sons for the sins of their fathers). Each shall die for his own sins". (Deut., 24:16).

How can they say that I am responsible for the transgressions of someone strange to me, someone whom I don't even know?

This is easily explained. The Talmud says in a Tractate *Kiddushin,* 40b):

"R. Elazar the son of R. Simon says "The world is judged according to the majority and the individual is judged according to the majority. Praiseworthy is someone who does a single *mitzvah* for he tilts the balances for himself and the entire world to the side of merit. Woe to him if he transgresses a single transgression for he tilts the balance for himself and the entire world to the side of guilt. As it is written 'And a single transgression causes a great loss.'"

Here R. Elazar the son of R. Simon has made me responsible for the entire world. For according to his opinion, all the people of the world are responsible for one another. Every individual, through his actions causes merit or guilt for the entire world. This is a very great surprise!

However, according to what we have explained above, the words of our Sages are understood and accepted very easily. For we have proven that each and everyone of the 612 *mitzvot* in the Torah centers around the single *mitzvah,* "Love Thy Friend As Thyself". And we have explained that this axis can be fulfilled only in a complete action where all its members are ready to do it.

CHAPTER 3

MUTUAL RESPONSIBILITY

(A continuation of the article "Giving of the Torah")
For all Israel are responsible for one another
TB Sanhedrin 27b, TB Shabuot 39a

All of Israel are responsible for one another for the Torah was not given to them until each and every one of them was asked if he agreed to accept upon himself the commandment of loving another at the level specified by the words "Love Thy Friend As Thyself".

Each and every Israelite was to accept upon himself to worry about and work for every member of the nation. He was to fulfill the other's needs no less than he would naturally look after his own. ,After the entire nation unanimously agreed and said "We will do and we will listen", then every Israelite became responsible that there should be nothing lacking to any member of the nation. Only then were they ready to receive the Torah and not before. With this mutual responsibility, every individual in the nation was relieved of his worries about his own personal needs. He could then keep the commandment of "Love Thy Friend As Thyself" to its fullest and give all he had to him who needed it. He no longer had to fear for his own existence for he knew and was ensured that 600,00 lovng, reliable people were around him and they stood prepared to worry about him. (See par. 16 in previous chapter).

For this reason, they were not at all ready to receive the Torah at the time of Abraham, Isaac and Jacob, but only when they left Egypt and became a nation complete unto themselves. Then came the reality that each one could be insured of all his needs without any worry or concern.

This was not the case when they were still intermingled with the Egyptians, and certainy not so when a certain portion of their needs were in the hands of those wild strangers who were filled with self-love. That portion in the hands of the Egyptians was totally uncertain for each individual Israelite. His friends could not fill these things he lacked, for it was not in their hands to do so.

We have already explained that when an individual is the least bit concerned for his own welfare, then he is unable to even begin fulfilling "Love Thy Friend As Thyself". It is now obvious that the giving of the Torah had to be delayed until the Egyptian exodus, until they became an independent nation, that is, until all their needs were in their own hands and not dependent on others. Then they were able to accept the mutual responsibility that we spoke of, and then they were given the Torah.

We find from this, that if, after giving the Torah, a few of the Israelites betrayed and returned to the filth of self-love without considering others, then to the degree to which they were depended upon, every individual must now be concerned for his own self, for those few will not have pity on him at all.

Of necessity then, no-one in Israel would fulfill the *mitzvah* of loving another. In this manner, those who throw off the yoke of fulfilling "Love Thy Friend As Thyself" cause those who observe the Torah to remain in their own filth of self-love. For they too are unable to engage in the *mitzvah* of "Love Thy Friend As Thyself" and to completely love another without their (the **betrayor's**) help, as we have said.

We see then that all of Israel are responsible for one another in both a positive and in a negative way. In a positive way, if they fulfill their responsibility until everyone worries about and fills the needs of his friends, then we find that everyone is able to keep the Torah and *mitzvot* completely, and they are able to do so to their Creator's satisfaction (as we said in paragraph 13). In a negative way, if a portion of the nation do not wish to keep the mutual responsibility, but are steeped in self-love, then they cause the rest of the nation to remain stuck in their filth and lowliness. They cannot find a way to escape their filthy stand, as we have explained.

18) The *Tanna* (Mishnaic Rabbi) explains the concept of mutual responsibility with two people on a ship. One of them began drilling a hole underneath himself and making a hole in the boat. His friend asked him why he was drilling? The man replied, "What difference does it make to you? I'm drilling under myself, not under you". The friend replied, "Fool! We will both die together in the ship". (Vayyira Rabba, Chapter 4).

This is what we have been saying. Because those who throw off the yoke are wallowing in self-love, they create by their actions a steel gate which prevents those who observe the Torah from even beginning to observe it as they should, that is, to the measure of "Love Thy Friend As Thyself", which is the ladder reaching upward to cleaving with Him.

And how correct the analogy is when he says, "Fool! We will both die together in the ship".

19) R. Elazar the son of R. Simon Bar Yochai differs still further on the issue of responsibility. It is not enough that all Israel are responsible for one another but the entire world enters together in this matter.

In reality, however, they don't differ. For all agree that, to begin with, it is sufficient for a single nation to keep the Torah. This is only the beginnning of the world's correction. For it was impossible to begin with all nations at one time. As they have said, "The L-rd went from one nation to another with his Torah and they didn't want to accept it". That is, they were wallowing in the filth of self-love to above their noses. There were those who engaged in illicit sexual relations or theft or murder. At that time, he would not even think of talking to them about withholding themselves from self-love.

Therefore, G-d found no nation that was capable of accepting the Torah except for the seed of Abraham, Isaac and Jacob. The merit of their forefathers stood on their behalf.

Our Sages said that our forefathers fulfilled the entire Torah even before it was given. The meaning is that due to the loftiness of their souls, they were able to perceive and come to the ways of G-d according to the spirituality of the Torah, which springs forth from cleaving to Him. They did not need the deeds prescribed in the Torah as a ladder to set for them a precedent. It was totally impossible for them to keep them (as we explained above in paragraph 16).

Without a doubt the physical unity and grandeur of our forefather's souls hold great influence on their succeeding generations. Their merit stood for that generation which received the Torah. Each and every member of the nation accepted upon himself this great obligation and each and every one said with full intent, "We will do and we will hear". This is the reason why we were chosen from among all other nations. We find, therefore, that only the Israelite nation entered into the desired responsibility, and none of the other nations of the world. This is simple, for it is true, and R. Elazar cannot disagree with it.

20) Completion of the world's rectification cannot be accomplished unless all people enter into the secrets of his service. As it is written (Zach 14:9) "And G-d will be th King of all the world; on that day will G-d be one and His name one." The Torah specified "on that day", and not before then. There are other similar scriptures, "For the land is full of the knowldge of G-d". (Jes. 11:9), "and all nations shall unto him" (Jes. 2:2).

The role of Israel relative to the other nations is similar to the role of our holy forefathers relative to the Israelite nation. That is, the merit of our forefathers enabled us to develop and purify ourselves until we were worthy of accepting the Torah. For had our forefathers not fulfilled the Torah before it was given, then we would not have been in the least superior to the other nations (see paragraph 19). Similarly, the Israelite nation must keep the Torah and *mitzvot* for their own sake to enable themselves and all mankind to develop and eventually accept upon themselves this exalted duty of loving another. This as we have said is the ladder to the purpose of creation which is cleaving unto Him.

With each and every *mitzvah* that an individual Israelite does for the satisfaction of his Creator and not for payment of some reward or self-love, he makes some degree of progress for all mankind. This transition cannot be done all at once but with slow stepwise progress until they add up to such a great sum that they are able to swing all mankind over to the desired purity.

This is what our Sage's statement of swinging to balance to the side of merit refers to. In the end, the desired amount of purity is attained. They compared it to one who has a balance scale where tipping the scale indicates the attainment of the desired weight.

21) This is the intent of R. Elazar the son of R. Simon Bar Yochai when he says that the world is judged according to the majority, etc. He refers to the task of the Israelite nation to purify the world to the desired level until all are worthy of accepting His work upon themselves. Their worthiness should be no less than that of the Israelites themselves when they received the Torah. In Rabbinic terms, this is called "having attained a majority of merits". The degree of purity must exceed the amount that they (the other nations) tilt to the balance to the side of demerit. It is understood that if the plate of merits, that is, the lofty understanding of loving another, is greater and exceeds the filty plate of demerit, then the nations become capable of conceding and agreeing. Then they can say "We will do and we will hear" just as the Israelites had done. Prior to this time, such cannot be the case. Prior to the time that they have a majority of merits, then the self-love forces them to refuse accepting His yoke.

This is the meaning of what they said:"Praiseworthy is he who does a single *mitzvah* for he swings the entire world to the side of merit." That is to say that in the end, the personal contribution of the individual Israeli combines with the total.

When a person is weighing sesame seeds, he continues adding one at a time until the weighing is completed. Every seed does its share in the weighing, for without it, the process would not be completed. The same can be said for the actions of an individual Israelite, they tilt the enire world to the side of merit. At the time that the weighing is completd and the balance for the entire world is on the side of merit, then each and every individual has a share in this weighing. For without his deeds, the necessary force would be lacking.

We now find that R. Elazar the son of R. Simon does not disagree with the rabbinical saying that all Israel is responsible for one another. Rather he is speaking about the rectification of the entire world for the future while our Sages are speaking of the present when only Israel has accepted the Torah for themselves.

22) The Bible says "and a single transgressor loses much good". (Eccl. 9:18) This supports the view of R. Elazar son of R. Simon. We have already explained above (par. 20) that the feeling of influence that reaches a person when he performs a commandment between man and G-d is precisely the same as that he receives when he performs one between man and his fellow man. He is obligated to perform all of them without the slightest trace of self-love. There is no light or hope of attaining reward or respect returning to him as a result of his toil. At this high point, love of G-d and love of his fellow man join and become one.

As we explained above (Par. 15), he is now causing a degree of progress on the ladder of loving another for all of mankind. His deeds, great or small, are added to those which tilt the balance of the world to the side of merit. His share takes part in the weighing (as we explained in par. 21).

One who commits a single transgression, that is, one who does not overcome his filthy self-love and thereby commits theft or the like, tilts the balance for himself and the entire world to the side of demerit. For when he reveals the filth of self-love, then the lowly nature of creation returns and is strengthened. As a result, he removes a certain amount from the final total on the plate of merit. This is similar to one who removes the single sesame seed that his friend had put there. As a result, the plate of merit rises just a little and he causes the world to regress.

This is what our Sages meant that "a single transgressor causes a great loss" (Ibid.). Because he was unable to restrain his miniscule desires he pushed the spirituality of the entire world backward.

23) What we said above (par. 5) is explained in these terms. The Torah was given specifically to the Israelite nation. There is also no doubt that arriving at the purpose of creation is required of all mankind — black, white or yellow — without any differentiation.

The nature of mankind had degenerated to such a low level, as we explained above. This is an issue of self-love which rules unbridled over all mankind. There was, therefore, no path or way to enter into discussion with them to explain that they should give in and accept, even the smallest degree, to exit the frame work of self-love which was causing difficulties for the world at large.

The Israelite nation was the exception to this. They had just undergone 400 years of slavery to the Egyptian nation with its great and awesome suffering. Our Sages tell us, "Just as salt sweetens the meat, so does suffering atone for a man's sins". It brings the body to a great degree of purification. In addition, the purity of their forefathers stood for them (as explained, par. 16). This is important and there are many scriptural passages to this effect.

By virtue of these two precedents, they were made capable of accepting the Torah. For this reason Scripture speaks of them in the singular as it is written, "And Israel camped there opposite the mountain." (Exodus 19:2). Our Sages commented that "They were as one person with a singular heart." Each and every individual completely removed from himself every trace of self-love. His entire purpose was to help his fellow man. We have proven this above (par. 16) when we explained the intent of the commandment Love Thy Friend As Thyself. Study this well!

We see then that all the individuals of the nation banded together and became a single heart and a single man.Only then were they capable of accepting the Torah, as we have explained.

24) The Torah was given specifically and only to the Israelite nation, the descendants of Abraham, Isaac and Jacob.One could not even think that a foreigner could participate with them. Because of this, the Israelite nation became a kind of pathway through whom the sparks of purification flow to all mankind. These sparks of purification accumulate daily as when one adds to a storehouse. The process continues until they reach the desired amount. At that time, mankind develops and reaches the point where they can appreciate the pleasure and rest that are contained in the kernel of loving another. Then they will know how to tilt the balance to the side of merit. They will come under His yoke and the plate of demerit will be burned out of this earth.

25) We must now complete what we explained in par. 16. The Torah was not given to our forefathers because the commandment of "Love Thy Friend As Thyself" cannot be carried out by individuals. This commandment is the central axis of the Torah and all the others revolve around it. It can only be observed with the prior agreement of an entire nation.

Giving of the Torah was therefore delayed until the Egyptian exodus, when they became capable of observing it. They were first asked if every member of the nation agreed to accept this commandment upon himself. After they agreed, they were given the Torah, as we have said.

26) We must still explain where we find in the Torah that the Israelites were asked this question and agree to it prior to accepting the Torah.

You should know that these things are obvious to all enlightened people. Prior to giving the Torah, G-d sent Moses to the Israelites. The Torah says, (Exodus 19, 5),

"And now if you will hearken unto my voice and keep my covenant, then you shall be unto me a special nation, for all the world is mine. And you shall be for me a kingdom of priests and a holy nation. These are the things which would shall say unto the children of Israel. And Moses came and he called the elders of the nation and placed before them all the things which G-d had commanded him. And all the nation together answered and said, 'We shall do all that G-d has said'. And Moses conveyed the words of the nation to G-d."

At first appearance, these things do not fit their purpose. Logic demands that if a person suggests to his friend that he do some work and he wants his approval, then he must give his friend an example of the work's content and its reward. Then the recipient can think about it and either refuse or agree.

In these two sentences, we don't, at first glance, find an example of the work or the reward for its performance. The Torah says, "if you will hearken unto my voice and keep my covenant." It does not explain what "my voice" or "my covenant" refer to. Afterwards, it says, "And you shall be unto me a special nation, for all the world is mine."

It is unclear from the context whether we are commanded to make an effort to be a special nation from among all the others or if this is a great promise to us. We must also understand the connection between this and the conclusion of the passage, "For all the world is mine."

The three Aramaic translations —— Onkelos, Yonathan ben Uziel, and Yerushalmi——and also the Biblical commentators—— Rashi, Ramban, etc.—— find it difficult to explain the literal meaning of this passage. *Ibn Ezra* brings, in the name of R. Merinos, that the word *"ki"* (usually interpreted as "for") means "in spite of the fact that." He explains that Israel shall be a special nation unto G-d in spite of the fact that all the world is G-d's. He (Ibn Ezra) thinks the same way himself.

This interpretation, however, does not fit the rabbinical saying that *"ki"* has four possible meanings —— either, lest, but, for. He (Ibn Ezra) is adding another meaning —— in spite of the fact that. Ibn Ezra then finishes the passage, "and you shall be unto me a nation of priests and a holy nation". Here too it is not clear from its content whether this is a commandment and we must make a special effort in this matter or if this is a good promise.

In addition, the phrase "a nation of priests" is not easily explained nor does it occur again anywhere in the Bible. We must especially define here some distinction between "a nation of priests" and "a holy nation". According to the common understanding of priesthood, it is synonymous with holiness. It is obviously understood that a kingdom composed entirely of priests is a holy nation. The words "holy nation" now become extraneous.

27) According to all that we have explained in this chapter, the passages can be properly explained. They are the image of a give and take, offer and acceptance with the phrases under discussion. He (G-d) is suggesting to them (the Israelites) the entire shape and content of the Torah and *mitzvot*, and the rewards that are due to its followers.

The form of the service in the Torah and commandments is expressed in the passage "and you shall be unto me a priestly nation". The meaning of a priestly nation is that each of you, young and old, will be like priests. Priests have no part of property or any physical possession on earth, for G-d is their portion. Similarly, the Israelite nation shall be so arranged that the world and everything that fills it will be holy for G-d. No individual shall work it any more than necessary to do G-d's service and fill the needs of others. No one's needs should be wanting. In this way, no individual need concern himself with his own needs, and in this way, even profane actions such as harvesting, planting and the like, have the identical character as the service of sacrifices which the priests due in the holy temple. What is the difference if I keep the commandment to bring a sacrifice to G-d, which is a positive precept, or if I keep the positive commandment of Love Thy Friend As Thyself? As a result, one who harvests his field so he can feed others is comparable to one who stands and brings a sacrifice to G-d. Not only this but we have shown above (parts 14, 15) that the commandment of Love Thy Friend As Thyself is more important than the bringing of a sacrifice.

We have still not completed the issue. The Torah and commandments were given to bring the Israelites together, that is to purify the body (see par 12 above). As a result of them, Israel merits the true reward, that of cleaving to G-d. This is the purpose of creation as we explained in par 6.

This reward is erxpressed in the words "a holy nation". As a result of cleaving to Him we become holy, as it is written in the Torah, "you shall be holy for I, the L-rd, your G-d, am holy". (Lev. 19:2).

We see that the words "a priestly nation" explains the type of service about the axis of Love Thy Friend As Thyself, that is, a nation composed entirely of priests where G-d is their portion and there is no personal property in the physical world.

We are forced to admit that this is the sole definition whereby we can understand this idea of "a priestly nation." We cannot explain it as referring to performing sacrifices on an altar, for this cannot be said of an entire nation. Who would be bringing the sacrifices? And as for giving gifts to the priests, who would be giving them? Similarly, we cannot explain it with respect to the holiness of the priest for it is written, "a holy nation".

It must be that the entire meaning of the phrase is that G-d is their share, and they have no personal physical possessions. This is the measure of Love Thy Friend As Thyself which includes, as we have said, the entire Torah with the words "a holy nation". The entire form of rewards, which is cleaving (to Him), is expressed.

28) We now fully understand the previous words, "And now if you will hearken to my voice and keep my covenant". They refer to making a covenant based on what I am now saying to you. "You shall be unto me a special nation", that is, you will be special unto me, for by your handiwork the sparks of bodily purification and refinement shall travel to all the nations of the world. For all the world's nations are not at all ready yet for this thing, and I need at least one nation to begin with at present to be special from all the other nations.

He therefore finishes with "For all the world is mine". That is to say that all nations belong to me, just as you do. In the end, they too shall cleave unto me (par. 20). But for now, when they are not yet capable of this task, I need a special nation. I now command you that "you shall be unto me a priestly nation", with the characteristic of loving another according to Love Thy Friend As Thyself which is the axis about which the Torah and commandments revolve. You shall also be "a holy nation". This is the reward in its final form of cleaving unto Me, and includes all possible reward which can be described.

Our Sages state this with their explanation of the conclusion, "these are the things which you shall tell the children of Israel." They specified, "these are the things', no more and no less". It is difficult to understand where they might think that Moses, our teacher, would add to or detract from G-d's words. Why would G-d have to warn him concerning this? We have no similar incident to this in the Torah. On the contrary, the Torah says about him, "in all my house he is trustworthy." (Numbers, 12:7).

29) From what has been said, it is well understood that, regarding the final character of the nature of the service

delineated in the words "priestly nation", which is the final definition of Love Thy Friend As Thyself, as it was possible for Moses to consider delaying and not revealing the nature of the service all at once in a single grand presentation out of fear that the Israelites might not agree to disown all physical possessions and give over all their wealth and property to G-d as implied in "a priestly nation."

This is similar to what Maimonides said that it is forbidden to reveal to women and children the fact that the correct way to perform the commandments is not for reward. One should wait until they mature and become wiser. Then they will be capable of carrying this out. We have discussed this above. G-d therefore pre-warned Moses "no less". Moses was to present to them the true nature, with all its lofty delineations as expressed in the words "a priestly nation".

It was also possible for Moses to consider explaining and expanding the sublime enjoyment and delight concealed in cleaving unto Him to draw them near so the Israelites would accept and agree to His great departure of withdrawing completely from all worldly possessions like priests. The warning was therefore issued, "no more".

Moses was to conceal and not elaborate on the entire issue of reward contained in the words "a holy nation." The reason is that if he were to reveal to them the wondrous departure in the quality of the reward, then they would certainly be confused and would accept His service solely to attain this great reward for themselves. This would be considered the same as one who is working for himself, for self-love. The whole intent would then be confounded as we have stated above (par. 13).

We have now explained that the phrase "no less" refers to the nature of the service contained in "a priestly nation". The phrase "no more" refers to the magnitude of concealed reward contained in "a holy nation".

CHAPTER 4

THE QUALITY AND GOAL OF RELIGION

Here I wish to answer three questions: (1) What is the essence of the (Jewish) religion? (2) Is its goal expected to be achieved in this world or specifically in the world to come? and (3) Is its goal for the betterment of the Creator or mankind?

At first glance, all who look at my topic will be astonished at the three questions I have chosen for myself as the topic for this chapter. For this is something elementary, and, besides, who doesn't know what religion is? And certainly its reward and punishment are expected (to be given) primarily in the world to come. And we needn't ask the third question, for everyone knows that its purpose is to direct mankind to good. So what can we add to this?

In truth, I have nothing at all to add. Most people know these three topics and are fluent in them since their youth. But, nothing has been added or explained since then. This shows a lack of understanding in these lofty areas. They are important because they are the foundation of the very structure on which religion is built.

Therefore, tell me! How is it possible that a lad of twelve or fourteen years already has the mental capacity to support and understand these three deep issues? Certainly he can't understand them sufficiently that he has no need to add more knowledge and wisdom for the rest of his life! So the issue is settled! For our quick supposition has led to a community with a sparse knowledge and to the wild conclusions that have filled the air in our generation. It has brought us to a condition in which the next generation has been practically lost.

THE ABSOLUTE GOOD

In order not to weary the reader with long expositions, I have relied on all that was written and explained in the previous chapters and especially on the chapter "Giving of the Torah." They serve as an introduction to the topic before us. Here I will speak succinctly and simply in order that all will understand.

Initially, we must understand that the Creator is "The Absolute Good". It is impossible that He caused someone to suffer even a little. This must be our first axiom.

The healthy mind clearly shows us that the basis for all who do evil is the "Desire to Receive." Because of their intense desire to receive to satisfy themselves, they find it by doing evil to another. As a result, evil is done to another because of the (doer's) "Desire to Receive" to satisfy himself. If no individual had any needs in society, then no one would do anything negative to another.

If we occasionally find someone who hurts another without any "Desire to Receive" self-satisfaction, then we know it is being done out of habit which itself developed from the "Desire to Receive". It is known that something done habitually does not require a new cause each time it is done.

We know that G-d is complete unto Himself. He needs no one to assist in His completion. He precedes everything. It is clear, then, that He has no "Desire to Receive." Since He has no characteristic of "Desire to Receive", then, perforce, He has no basis for doing evil to anyone. This is sheer simplicity.

Another axiom which we can accept is that He has a Desire to Impart good to others, that is, to His creatures. This, too, is sheer simplicity, and is proven to us from the great creation which He created and arranged for us.

After it is clearly and completely known that it is not within G-d's nature to do evil, as we have explained, then it must be that all creatures receive only good from Him, for He created them solely to do good for them. We conclude that He has a desire to impart only good. In no way in the world can there be in His nature any reason why damage or pain might issue from Him. For this reason, we have defined Him with the name "The Absolute Good." Now that we know this, we will look at the actual reality which is directed by Him, and how He imparts them only good.

HIS SUPERVISION IS A GOAL-ORIENTED ONE

This is understood on the basis of the natural order arranged before our eyes. Every small creation, such as it may be, is of one of four types: Silent, Growing, Alive, Speaking (Inanimate, Plant, Animal, Human). This is true in both a general and a specific way. They have a goal-oriented supervision, that is, a slow, stepwise growth with a "cause and effect" development.

A fruit on a tree is an example. It is supervised in such a way that in the end it is attractive and pleasant tasting. Ask a botanist the number of stages a fruit must undergo from the time it first appears until it finally ripens, thus completing its purpose. All the stages which precede its purpose bear no resemblance to its final state. Rather, as if to anger us, it shows us the exact opposite situation. The sweeter a fruit is in its final stage, the more bitter and uglier it is in its developing stages.

The same is true of living creatures and humans. The animal with limited adult intelligence has a few difficulties along the course of its development. Man, by comparison, has a high intelligence when he reaches maturity. He has greater difficulties during his development. A newborn calf is still called an ox. It has strength and a self-preservation instinct. It can stand on its own feet and walk about, and it can avoid obstacles in its way. This is not true of a newborn human. It lays by itself and behaves as if it had lost its senses. Someone not experienced in the ways of this world, upon looking at these two infants would certainly say that the human child would never amount to anything. The animal offspring's future would be compared to a second Napoleon.

This is so if we judge according to the degree of wisdom of the calf compared with that of the newborn human. The human child appears stupid and senseless. Here we clearly see that His supervision over His creatures is surely a "goal-oriented supervision". We see this even without taking into account the ordered stages of development. For, on the contrary, they deceive us and prevent us from understanding their true purpose. Their state is always opposite their final one.

In areas like these we say that experience is the best teacher, for only an experienced person who has had the opportunity to see the creature in all phases of its development through its final completion can relax and not fear at all from all the negative stages that it had during its development. He believes that in its ripened stage it will be beautiful and clear. (The reason that all creatures go through these ordered stages is well explained in the Kabbalah. This is not the place to expand on it).

We have now explained the ways of His supervision in our world. It is solely a goal-oriented supervision. The measure of its good is not at all obvious until the creature reaches its final point; the point at which it assumes its final shape and maturity. On the contrary, it usually appears tainted to those who look at it.

Before our eyes we see that G-d continuously imparts only good to His creation. This good is directed from His by way of the "goal-oriented supervision."

TWO WAYS –– THE WAY OF SUFFERING, AND THE WAY OF TORAH

We have already explained that G-d is the Absolute Good. He watches over us with His complete goodness without any admixture of evil. He does this through his goal-oriented supervision, which forces us to accept a series of differing circumstances obeying the laws of cause and effect. This continues until we are capable of receiving the desired good, at which time we will come to our goal. This is just like the beautiful fruit when it completely matures.

With this it is understood that this goal is promised to us, to all of us, absolutely! If this were not the case, then there would be a flaw in His providence, and it would not be sufficient for its purpose, G-d forbid! Our Sages have said, that the Divine presence dwells with the lower creatures to fulfill a higher purpose. His supervision is goal-oriented and it is directed to bringing us to cleaving unto Him so that in the end He may dwell in our midst. This is thought of as a higher purpose. This is as if to say that if we do not reach this (goal) then there is

(G-d forbid) some blemish in His providence.

It is similar to a great king who, while very old, had a son. He loved the child very much. From the day the child was born, the king thought about his well being. He gathered all the fine books and all the wise men in the country. He prepared for his son a place to study wisdom. The king sent for all the famous builders and built his son palaces for pleasure. He gathered musicians and instruments; he built concert halls. He called the best bakers and chefs to prepare for him all the sweetest things in the world.

The child grew and matured. He was a fool and was not interested in being enlightened. He was blind and could not see nor appreciate the beauty of the buildings. He was deaf and couldn't hear the voice of the singers or the instruments. He was a diabetic and could only eat coarse bread. It caused the king great anger and distress.

Circumstances like these can happen to a king of flesh and blood. But the same cannot be said about G-d. The idea of falsity does not apply to Him.

G-d, therefore, prepared for us two paths for development. The first is the path of suffering, this is the path of development of the creature from within. It must, according to natural law, operate according to the principle of cause and effect in different circumstances occurring one after another. Through this means we slowly develop until we arrive at the stage of being able to choose the good and to hate the evil. Finally we reach the destined ability which He desires. This path takes a long time and is filled with suffering and pain.

G-d therefore prepared for us a very pleasant path. This is the path of the Torah and commandments which can make us capable of our purpose quickly and without suffering. What derives from this is the final goal of our being capable of cleaving to Him so that He may dwell in our midst. This goal is obligatory, without any deviation.

His supervision of us is strong in both its forms –– the path of suffering and the path of Torah. Because of the practical reality, we find that His supervision comes to us simultaneously from both paths. Our Sages called them, "the way of the world, and the way of Torah."

THE ESSENCE OF RELIGION TO DEVELOP WITHIN US THE SENSE OF RECOGNIZING EVIL

Our Sages have said, "what difference does it make to God if we slaughter from the throat or from the nape? We see that the *mitzvot* were given for the sole purpose of bringing mankind together." (Bereshit Rabba, Chapter 44). We have previously discussed this in the second chapter (par. 12). The reader is referred there.

Here I will explain the essence of this development which is realized by engaging in the Torah and *mitzvot*. One should know that this refers to a (person's) recognition of the evil within him. Engaging in the *mitzvot* is capable of purifying one via a slow stepwise process. The measure of these steps of purification is the degree to which a person recognizes the evil within him.

Man is, by his very nature, already capable of pushing all evil away from and burning it out of himself. All mankind has an equal ability in this regard. The difference between one creature and another lies in the recognition of evil. A more developed creature recognizes evil much better and perforce separates and forces the evil out of itself to a greater degree. A less developed creature recognizes less evil within itself and will therefore push away only a smaller amount of evil. It leaves within itself a greater degree of foulness for it does not at all recognize it as such.

In order not to weary the reader, we will explain the principles of good and evil. We explained in the second chapter (par. 12) that evil is nothing more than self-love, also called "egoism." Its form is the opposite of the Creator who has absolutely no Desire to Receive for himself alone. He seeks only to impart. We also explained there (pars. 9 & 11) that the whole idea of pleasure and enjoyment is proportional to the degree that the creature imitates his Creator. The idea of suffering and impatience are essentially relative to the degree of differing from the Creator. Egoism is therefore despicable and painful because it is the opposite of our Creator.

The degree of despising evil is not the same in all people. A wild, totally undeveloped person does not recognize egoism as a negative trait at all. He uses it without any embarrassment or limit, openly stealing and killing at any opportunity. One who is slightly developed already recognizes a degree of evil in his egoism. He is at least embarrassed to display it in public. He will not steal or kill where there are witnesses, but will still carry out these intentions where no man will see him.

Someone still more developed realizes that egoism is something completely despicable to the point that he cannot at all withstand it as a part of him. He pushes it away and separates himself from it to the degree that he recognizes it. This continues to the point where he does not wish to benefit from the toil of others.

At this time the sparks of loving another, which we call altruism, begin arousing within him. This is an all-encompassing good trait. Altruism develops within him in a stepwise fashion. In the beginning he develops a feeling of love and a desire to impart to fill the needs of his friends and family. On this, the Torah says, "and you shall not ignore your own flesh" (Isaiah 58:7). As he develops further, this trait of imparting increases within him to include the others in his city or his nation. This continues until he develops a love for all of mankind.

INTENTIONAL AND UNINTENTIONAL DEVELOPMENT

You should know that there are two forces which force us to climb the rungs of the ladder we have described. They push us until we reach its top in heaven. This is the goal wherein we imitate our Creator.

The difference between the two forces is that one pushes us without our knowledge, that is, whether we want it or not. This force pushes us from behind (with a "turge"). This corresponds to what we have called the way of suffering or the way of the world. The philosophy of *"Musar"*, or ethics, derives from this force. It is based upon experience, through critical analysis of practical matters.

The entire essence of this body of knowledge is merely a summary of the damages which our eyes witness, damages caused by egoism. The experiences are haphazard and come our way without our knowledge or choice. They are, however, true to their goal, for the images of evil can be experienced through our senses. We avoid the damages to the degree that we are able to recognize them. In this way we rise to a higher rung on the ladder.

The second force draws with our knowledge for it operates through our free will. This force pulls us from before us (with a "front"). This corresponds to what we have called the way of Torah and *mitzvot*. By engaging in *mitzvot*, and doing service for the satisfaction of our Creator, the facility of recognizing evil develops within us with amazing speed. This has already been explained in Chapter 2 (par. 13).

Our benefit is twofold. Firstly, we needn't wait for life's experiences to push us from behind. These pushes are measured in terms of the suffering and destruction caused to us because of the presence of evil in our midst. On the other hand, through service to God, we develop this recognition without having to first suffer and be destroyed. On the contrary, through the pleasure and enjoyment that we feel when we serve G-d in purity, to satisfy Him, we develop a (system of) relative values. Through this system we recognize how the lowly sparks of self love interfere with our receiving the taste of the pleasure of G-d's influence.

The sense of recognizing evil develops within us at times of pleasure and great peace of mind. It comes when we receive the good as we serve G-d. We then feel the pleasure and satisfaction that derives to us from imitating our Creator.

The second benefit is time. This method works with our complete knowledge. We have the ability to increase service in the Torah and thereby increase (our learning) to any rate we desire.

Religion is Not For The Benefit of the Creations But For the Benefit of Him Who Performs the Service.

There are many who mistakenly compare our holy Torah to the principles of ethics. They do so because they have never in their lives experienced the taste of religion. I call upon them with the Scripture, "Taste and see that G-d is good" (Psalms 34:9).

In truth, both religion and ethics have the same intent. They both strive to elevate man from the limiting filth of self-love and to bring him to the pinnacle of loving others. In spite of all this, however, they are as far apart from one another as the intentions of G-d are from the intentions of man. Religions stem from the thoughts of G-d and the principles of ethics from the thoughts of people and their life experiences.

The difference between them is therefore obvious. They differ on all practical points and also in their final goal. The recognition of evil and good that develops within us when we practice the principles of ethics is relative to success of the community, as is well known. Such is not the case with religion. The recognition of good and evil that develops within us through its practice is relative only to God. We differentiate between man being different from his Creator and man imitating his Creator. The latter is called "cleaving" as we have explained in the second chapter (pars. 9, 10, & 11).

They are also far from one another with regard to their goal. The goal of the ethical principles is for the welfare of the community. They (the goals) are taken from practical analysis of life's experiences. In the end, the goal does not promise its followers any benefit above the natural framework. For this reason, the goal continues to be analyzed. After all, who can prove to an individual the final measure of good he receives in such a way that he is convinced that he must limit his self-image to some degree for the sake of the community?

This is not the case with the goal of religion. It promises

benefit to the very person who engages in it. We have already proven that when a person comes to love others that he is cleaving to G-d; he is imitating his Creator. By cleaving, he goes from his narrow, painful, plague-filled world to the wide everlasting world filled with imparting to G-d and imparting to His creatures.

There is also an obvious difference with regard to the supporting structure of these systems. Work done according to the ethical principles is based upon finding favor in the eyes of mankind. This is similar to a reward which is paid at the end (of the service). When a person becomes habituated to this kind of work, he is unable to elevate himself on the stairways of ethics. He is already used to the kind of service where he receives handsome rewards from his surroundings for his good deeds.

This is not the case when service of Torah and mitzvot is done for the Creator's satisfaction without receiving any reward. One rises above the level of ethics in proportion to the work done. He receives no reward along his path. As each and every cent adds up to a large sum, (his rewards add up) until he acquires a second nature of imparting to others without any desires of receiving for himself, except that which he needs to live.

We find, then that he is truly liberated from all the restrictions of creation. For when a person despises all personal acquisitions and his soul is repelled by all unimportant excessive physical pleasures, respect, etc., then he freely strolls in the world of G-d. He is assured that no worldly harm shall come to him. For all harm is brought upon a person only because of the selfishness which is naturally within him. This must be well understood.

We have thoroughly explained that the goal of religion is entirely for the purposes of the person who engages in it. It is not at all for the benefit of the community even though all of a person's actions revolve around benefitting the community and are gauged by this standard. But this is nothing more than a transition stage to the grand goal of imitating the Creator.

We now understand that the reward of religion is collected in this world, as a person lives a life we have been describing. (The reader should carefully study the second chapter, par. 6 regarding the general and specific goals). The issue of reward in the world to come is a separate one and I will explain it in its own article. (PUBLISHER'S NOTE: We have not merited to receive this article. The reader is directed to the introduction to Talmud *Esser Sfirot*, paragraph 76 and to chapter 7, par. 10. See also *Panim Meirot*, chapter 11, page 68).

CHAPTER 5

THE ESSENCE OF KABBALISTIC WISDOM

Before I begin explaining the implications of Kabbalistic wisdom, as many before me have done, I felt it necessary to first thoroughly explain the essence of this wisdom. It is my opinion that very few know what it is. Obviously we cannot speak about the implications of something until we understand the thing itself.

The subject is as vast and deep as the sea. In spite of this, I will make a great effort and use all the knowledge I have acquired in this area to present basic explanations and enlighten the subject from all angles. It will be sufficient for all readers to come to the correct and true conclusions. I will leave no room for the reader to make a mistake as they often do when they study these subjects.

WHAT DOES THIS WISDOM REVOLVE AROUND?

This question no doubt occurs to all intelligent people. To sufficiently answer the question, I will give a safe reliable definition:

"This wisdom is no more and no less than the order of roots which concentrate according to the laws of cause and effect. (They do so) according to fixed absolute rules. They combine and hit the target of a single supernal purpose which is called 'the revelation of His Godliness to His creatures in this world.'"

This pertains to both mankind in general and to individuals. In general, we can say that in the end, all of mankind must, of absolute necessity, come to this degree of development (of cleaving to God). The Torah says, "For the earth is filled with knowlege of G-d, even as the waters cover the seas" (Isaiah 11:9), "No longer will each man teach his friend and his brother knowledge of G-d for all of them, young and old, shall know Me" (Jer. 31:34), and "And your Teacher shall no longer hide Himself and your eyes shall see your Teacher" (Isaiah 30:20).

Individually, even before all of mankind reaches this stage of completion, there will be some special people in every generation to whom this will apply. These individuals merit a certain degree of G-d-consciousness. They are the prophets and people of special repute. Our Sages have said (*Bereshit Rabba*, chapter 74), "There is no generation in which we do not have men like Abraham, Isaac and Jacob". Here we see that G-d-consciousness is present in every generation, for our Sages are authorities in this area and we can trust them.

MANY COUNTENANCES, SFIROT AND WORLDS

According to what we have stated, a question arises. Since this wisdom has only one specific purpose, how then can there be so many countenances and *Sfirot* and so many variable connections? Kabbalistic books are full of these topics.

The answer can be found in nature. Take, for instance, the body of any small living creature, one whose sole purpose is to nourish itself so that it can live in this world long enought to reproduce and perpetuate its species. We see in it a complicated combination of millions of capillaries and veins. Physiologists and anatomists have confirmed this. There are also tens of millions which are as yet unseen by the human eye. From this we can extrapolate how many combinations of channels and things are necessary to understand the creature in its entirety (lit. this lofty purpose).

TWO ORDERS: TOP DOWN AND BOTTOM UP

This wisdom is divided into two orders which parallel one another and are as similar as two drops of water. There is no difference between them. The first one draws from above (heaven) down to this world. The second begins in this world and goes upward. It uses the same paths and combinations which were recorded when they first appeared at their roots and were revealed from above downward. The first order is called, in Kabbalsitic terms, the order of concatenation of the worlds, countenances, and *Sfirot*. This is true whether they (the worlds, etc.) are fixed or variable.

The second order is called comprehensions or levels of prophecy and Divine Inspiration. One who merits them must go through the same paths and attain every specific point in every level. He does so slowly and precisely. He proceeds according to the rules laid down when they were emanated downward from above. This is so because revelation of His Godliness does not appear at once as do physical things. Instead, it appears only with the passage of time according to the purity of the one who comprehends it. In the end, all the many levels and arrangements from above down are revealed to him. They are ordered and are comprehended one after another, in a manner that each comprehended level is higher than the other, similar to a ladder.

For this reason they are called levels.

ABSTRACT NAMES

Many are of the opinion that all the words and names used in Kabbalah are a type of abstract names. This is because Kabbalah is involved with G-dliness and spirituality. These subjects are above time and space and even the imagination cannot grasp them. For this reason, many feel that any names referring to these (Kabbalistic) topics must be abstract or on an even higher and grander level than abstract, for the names have absolutely nothing to do with anything we can imagine.

Not only is this not true, but the exact opposite is true. Kabbalah uses the names and attributes only for their realistic and practical value. It is an iron-clad rule among all Kabbalists that "we cannot define with words anything of which we cannot conceive."

Here, it is important to know that the word *"Hassagah"* (conception) refers to the final level of understanding. It is used in the manner of *"tassig yadekha"* (your hand shall be able to acquire). Until something is totally clear and understood (in the mind), just as it is grasped in the hand, the Kabbalists do not use the word *"Hassagah"* but rather understanding, enlightenment, etc.

THE TANGIBLE IN KABBALAH

In the real, physical world of our senses, there are tangible things whose essence we neither understand nor can we imagine. Examples include electricity and magnetism which we called fluids. Who would claim that the names used for these items are not real? We fully recognize how they work, and we don't care at all that we have no grasp of their essence, that is, of the electron itself.

The name is very real and close to us. It is almost as if we fully understood it. Even little children recognize the name "electricity" just as they recognize the words "bread," "sugar," etc.

If you wish to tax your mind, think of the following generality. We cannot understand or grasp the Creator in even the smallest way. The same is true with all of His creatures, including those physical ones we can feel with our hands. Everything that we recognize in this world, including our friends and relatives is nothing more than a recognition of the outcomes that develop when our senses interact with them. This totally suffices us in spite of the fact that we have no grasp of the essence of the issue.

Moreover, you don't even comprehend your own essence. Everything that you know about your own essence is based on the outcome of your actions.

You can now easily understand that all the names and expressions appearing in Kabbalistic works are also real and tangible. This is true even though we have no comprehension of their meaning. Those who utilize the names fully and completely recognize them in their entirety. That is, they know the things that are accomplished and result from the interaction of the supernal light with our comprehensions of it. This much is enough.

The principle may be stated tersely: "Everything meted out and emanating from His providence which manifests in the natural world is precisely sufficient (for the world's needs)." For example, no person would claim a need for a sixth finger because five exactly suffice him.

PHYSICAL PROPERTIES AND BODILY NAMES IN KABBALISTIC BOOKS

Every logical person understands that when we are involved with something spiritual, not to mention with God, there are no words or letters to contemplate on. Our entire vocabulary is made up of combinations of letters of the imagination and senses and they cannot help us when words relating to the imagination and senses do not apply.

Take, for example, the most concrete term that we can which pertains to this subject, "supernal light" or even "simple light." This is an artificial thing, borrowed from the light of the sun or from a candle or the light of satisfaction that a person feels when he discovers the answer to a doubtful issue. How can we use these words when speaking of spiritual matters or the ways of G-d? The words only suggest lies and falsities. This is certainly true in areas when we must use these words to reveal some idea in the give and take that customarily occurs in Kabbalistic studies. At those times, the Kabbalist must be very precise and stay within absolute boundaries so as not to confuse the readers. Should the Kabbalist be caught with even a single unsuccessful word, then he will confuse his readers. They will not understand what precedes the word, what follows it, and everything connected with that word. This is well known to all who study Kabbalistic books.

It should surprise you then how the Kabbalists use false words to explain the relationships that exist within Kabbalah. It is known that false words have no precise definition for lies have no legs to stand on. To understand, we must first know the law of root and branch as it pertains to the interrelationships of the worlds.

LAW OF ROOT AND BRANCH IN THE RELATIONSHIP BETWEEN THE WORLDS

Kabbalists have found that there are four similar worlds. Their names are Emanation, Creation, Formation and Action. *(Atzilut, Beriah, Yetzirah, Asiyah)*. The first world is the highest and is called Emanation. Our world of the physical and sensual is called Action.

The shape of these worlds is identical in all aspects and particulars. All things found or occurring in the first world are also found in the second world which is beneath it. There is absolutely no change. The same is true of the rest of the worlds after it, until we arrive at our physical world. The only difference between the worlds is one of level. This manifests in the substance contained in the particulars found in each and every world. The substance in the particular things found in the first, highest world is purer than in all the worlds beneath it. The substance of the particulars in the second world are denser than in the first world, but purer than that of everything on levels below it.

It continues in this manner until we reach our world. The substance of the particulars contained in it are the most dense and darkest of all the worlds which precede it. The shape of the particulars found in it and all their occurrences are identical qualitatively and quantitatively in all the worlds without any change.

The Kabbalists have compared this to a stamp and the thing stamped by it. All the shapes that we found on the stamp are transferred entirely with all their specifics to the item stamped by it. So it is with our worlds. Every lower world is stamped from the one above it. Therefore, all the forms that are present in the upper world are copied quantitatively and qualitatively in their entirety. They come to the lower world in a way that there is no detail or occurrence in the lower world which does not have its counterpart in the world above it. Their shapes are as identical as two drops of water.

This is called "root and branch." The specific entity found in the lower world is like a branch of its counterpart in the upper world. The upper entity is the root of the lower entity, because the lower entity is formed and comes into existence from it.

This is the intention of our Sages when they say that "every blade of grass has a *mazal* (star, fortune) and a keeper above which strikes it and tells it to grow" (Omissions from the Zohar, Genesis, par. 1; Genesis Rabbah, chap. 10). The root, which is here called *mazal* forces it to grow and acquire its quantitative and qualitative characteristics. This is identical to the stamp and thing stamped we mentioned above.

This is the law of root and branch. It applies to all the specifics of our reality and all occurrences in every world in relation to the one above it.

THE LANGUAGE OF KABBALISTS IS THE LANGUAGE OF BRANCHES

The Kabbalistic language is based upon what the branches, which are the examples of the roots in the upper worlds, reveal to us. There is nothing in the lower world which does not derive from the world above it according to the paradigm of stamp and thing stamped, as we have discussed above. The root on the upper world forces the branch in the lower world to reveal its shape and contents, as our Sages have said. The *mazal* in the upper world associated with the grass in the lower world strikes the grass and forces it to grow as it should. In this way, every branch in our world clearly defines its image in the upper world.

For this reason the Kabbalists have a sufficient specific vocabulary available. It can be used for spoken communication and fully excels for the task. Using it, they can discuss with one another the spiritual roots in the upper worlds. They refer to the lower physical branch in this world which is well defined to our physical senses. The listener understands the upper root on his own. He knows that the lower branch describes it because the two are associated, the lower being stamped from the upper.

In this manner, all the specifics and occurrences of our physical creation become defined as absolute words and names for the upper spiritual roots. This is so in spite of the fact that in their spiritual place they are beyond the imagination and cannot be described with any words. But because of their branches in our sensual world, they have acquired the merit of description through words.

This is the nature of the language spoken among Kabbalists. Via the language, the spiritual comprehensions are revealed from person to person in succeeding generations. They understand one another perfectly whether communicating by mouth or in writing. The degree of precision needed for a Kabbalistic study is attained. It is impossible to stumble because every branch has a precise natural definition unique to itself. It also describes its root in the upper world according to its precise definition.

One should know that it is easier to explain all the concepts of Kabbalah using the language of branches than with any other language. We know this from the study of nominalism (semantics?). The public becomes confused in their use of language. That is, because they use them so frequently, the words lose their original meaning. As a result, great difficulties arise in conveying precise ideas from one person to another, whether orally or in writing.

This is not so with the language of branches of the Kabbalah. It is taken from the names of creatures and their occurrences. These are ordered and appear before our eyes well defined by natural laws. They are immutable forever. One who hears or reads them can never misunderstand the words used becasue the natural laws are absolute and unchangeable.

TRANSMISSION FROM A KABBALISTIC SAGE TO A STUDENT WHO UNDERSTANDS BY HIMSELF

Nachmanides in his introduction to his Torah commentary and similarly, Rabbi Hayyim Vital, in his Ma'amar Pesi'ot wrote, "The reader should know that no one will understand even a word contained in these Kabbalistic works except for a wise person who receives the teaching orally from a Kabbalist and is able to understand on his own."

Our Sages have said that "we do not expound on the Chariot to individuals unless they are wise and understand on their own." (TB Chagigah, 13b). We understand from this that one must receive the teaching from a Kabbalist. But what of this requirement that the student must also be wise and understanding in his own right, and if he is not, then even if he is the most righteous person in the world, it is forbidden to teach him? Moreover, if he is wise and understanding on his own, then he has no need to learn from others.

From what has been said above, we can easily understand this. We explained that all the words and expressions we utter cannot explain even a single word of the spiritual, G-dly things which are above time and space. We have instead a special language for these things. It is the language of branches according to their relations to the upper roots. This language, as we said above, is very much more suitable for purposes of give and take in Kabbalistic studies than normal languages. But this is true only if the listener is himself wise, that is, he knows and understands the relationships between the branches and their roots.

These relationships are not at all explained from the bottom up. That is, if one looks at the lower branches, it is impossible to draw any analogy or likeness to any form in the upper roots. In fact, the opposite is true – he learns the lower from the upper. From the outset, he must comprehend the upper roots as they exist in their unimaginable spirituality. His comprehension must be pure. (See the Tangible in Kabbalistic Wisdom).

After he understands the upper roots well, he can now look at the perceptible branches in this world. He knows how each branch relates to its root in the upper world according to its orders, quantity and quality. After he knows and understands this well, then there is a common language between his teacher and him. This is the language of the branches. Through it (the language), the Kabbalistic Sage can give over to him (the student) all the Kabbalistic studies that pertain to the upper spiritual worlds. This includes what he obtained from his teachers plus what he himself has found to expand Kabbalah. Then they have a common language between them and they understand one another.

As long as a student is not wise and does not understand the language and the relationship between branches and roots, then, clearly, the Rabbi cannot explain to him one single word of this spiritual wisdom. Certainly they cannot discuss and study Kabbalah, for they don't have a common language to use. They are like two mutes. Perforce, then, we do not teach him the Workings of the Chariot, which is itself the Kabbalistic Wisdom, unless he is wise and understands on his own.

We may ask another question. How did the student become wise enough that he understands the relationships between branch and root through investigation of the upper roots? The answer is that one must have G-d's help for he has no chance without it. G-d fills those whom He favors with wisdom, understanding and knowledge to be enlightened with higher comprehensions. One cannot be helped in this by a person of flesh and blood. Therefore, after he has found favor in G-d's eyes and merits a higher comprehension, then he is ready to come and receive the vastness of Kabbalistic wisdom orally from a Kabbalistic Sage. Now they have a common language. There is no other way.

NOMENCLATURE FOREIGN TO THE HUMAN SPIRIT

With what we have explained above, you can understand that in Kabbalistic books, there frequently occur expressions and nomenclature that are foreign to the human spirit. They are most prevalent in the basic books including the Zohar, Tikkunim and the writings of the Ari. It is very surprising. Why did these Sages use these lowly expressions to express these grand and holy ideas? But with the knowledge presented above, you properly understand this. We explained that it is absolutely impossible to explain Kabbalah with any worldly language. A special language is needed and that is the language of the branches. It is based on the relationships to the upper roots.

It is self-evident, therefore, that it is impossible to exclude any branch or its occurrence because it is on a low level. We must use it to express the desired idea within the framework of Kabbalah. This is so because we have no other branch in our world to take in its place. Just as no two hairs grow from the same follicle, no two branches relate to the same root. If we leave out one occurrence and don't utilize it, then, not only do we lose this spiritual idea in the upper world, for we have no other word to susbtitute to show this root, but this also damages the entire Wisdom and all that surrounds it. We have lost one link in the chain of wisdom that is connected to that concept. In the end, we are blemishing the entire Kabbalah, for there is no other worldly wisdom where the subjects are united and tied together by cause and effect, like the Kabbalah. From its beginning to its end, it is tied together, just like a long chain. So if we lose one small piece of knowledge in the middle, the entire wisdom is obscured because all its topics are strongly tied to one another and combined into a single unit.

Now there is no surprise why the Sages occassionally use foreign expressions. They don't have the freedom to choose expressions and to exchange good and bad ones. They must always bring precisely that branch or occurrence which delineates the upper root exactly as needed. They must also expand the subject so their friends who are studying it will have a precise definition.

PART TWO

THE ROOTS IN KABBALAH

CHAPTER 6

SUBSTANCE AND FORM IN KABBALAH

Science in general has two divisions: The first is called the knowledge of substance and the second is called knowledge of form. There is nothing in the world which does not consist of substance and form. For example, a table has substance —— wood —— and form —— the shape of a table. The substance, wood, constitutes the form which is the table. Similarly, the word 'liar.' It has substance —— a person —— and form —— the lie. The substance, which is the person, constitutes the form of falsehood. The person habitually lies. The same is true of all things.

The science which deals with the specific things found in reality, is also divided into two divisions: The knowledge of substance, and the knowledge of form. That division which deals with the nature of the substance of things, with or without taking their form into account, is called the knowledge of substance. This knowledge is based on experience, that is, on proofs and analogies taken from practical experience. These experiences are taken as an assured basis for their conclusions which are assumed to be true.

The second division of science deals with abstract shapes of substances without concerning itself with the substances themselves. They eliminate the aspects of truth or falsehood in the shape of the substance for they (the scientists) define these qualities. The scientists deal solely with the values of importance or lack thereof in these forms of truth and falsehood, such as they may be, each according to its own bare essence, as if they were not encompassed by any substance. This is called knowledge of form.

This knowledge is not based on any practical experience, for abstract forms like these do not enter into practical experience. They are not part of practical reality. An abstract form is taken solely from the imagination. Only the imagination can form it for it is not practical reality. Therefore, all scientific knowledge of this type is built solely upon the basis of speculation. It is not taken from practical experience, but solely from the give and take of speculation. All higher philosophy is of this type. Therefore, a large portion of the modern thinkers have abandoned it. They are not satisfied with give and take built on speculation. In their opinion, it is an uncertain basis. They consider only a practical basis as certain. This is well known.

Kabbalah is also divided into the same two categories: The study of substance and the study of form. But there is a major distinction between it and profane science —— in Kabablah, even the study of form is built entirely upon a study of practical understanding, that is, on a basis of practical experience.

CHAPTER 7

PEACE

SUBTITLE: A PRACTICAL SCIENTIFIC STUDY ON THE
OBLIGATION TO SERVE G-D

"And the wolf shall dwell with the lamb and the leopard shall
lie down with the kid; and the calf and the young lion and
the fatling together; and a little child shall lead them" (Is.
11:6).

"And on that day the L-rd will set His hand again a second
time to recover the remnant of His people that shall remain
from Assyria and from Egypt, and from Patros and Cush and
from Elam and from the islands of the sea" (Isaiah 11:11).

Rabbi Simon B. Halafta said, "God did not find any vessel
capable of holding blessing for Israel except peace. As it is
written (Ps. 29:11) 'G-d shall give might to His nation, G-d
shall bless His nation with peace.'" (TB Uktzin, end).

I have explained the general form of serving G-d in the previous
chapters as being no more and no less than loving others. From
a practical viewpoint, this can be defined as imparting to others.
When we consider loving another as part of an action, every
action is then described in terms of imparting good to another.
We may now define loving others as imparting to others. This
term is more capable of insuring that we will not forget the
intent.

Now that we know how to serve Him properly, we must determine whether we must accept this service on faith only, without any practical scientific basis or if we also have a practical basis for this. This is what I want to prove in the present chapter.

From the outset, I must completely prove the subject itself, that is, who is it who receives our service? I do not love the philosophy of form. I hate all types of inquiries that are built on specualtion. And it is known that the majority of my generation agrees with me on this matter. We retract from these types of bases for they are shattered foundations. If the foundation should shake, the whole structure will fall. Therefore, I shall not say a single word that is not based on a study of understanding gained through experience. I will begin with things that are easily recognized without dispute and I will continue proving, in an analytical* way, until we prove the existence of (the upper subject) (G-d). From this perspective we will come back, and, using a synthetic** analysis, arrive at how serving Him is proven through a practical understanding of reality.

OPPOSITION AND CONTRADICTION IN PROVIDENCE

Every intelligent person who looks at reality finds two things totally opposite of one another. If one looks at the order of creation from the aspect of its existence and structure, it is

---

* Analytical: Separation of a thing into all of its aspects
** Synthetic: Combination and connection between things such as analogy and inference from minor to major

obvious that there is a confirmed direction, guided by deep wisdom and capability. This applies to the existence of the various categories of reality and to the general assurance of its continued existence.

Take for example the sequence of events in a person's coming into existence. The love and the pleasure of the parents is prepared as a starting point. It is certain and true to its task. And when the drop of semen leaves the father's organ, providence has prepared for it a secure place, arranged with great wisdom. It is capable of receiving the spirit of life. There, providence provides it with the necessary nutrients on a daily basis, precisely as needed. It also prepared for it a wonderful recepticle in its mother's womb in a manner that nothing foreign can injure it.

Providence takes care of all its needs, just like an experienced governess. Providence does not forget it for a moment until it acquires the power and strength to exit into our world. At that time, providence gives it temporary strength and vigor sufficient to break through the walls that surround it. Just like a tested, armed warrior, it proceeds and creates for itself an opening through which to exit to the world.

Even then providence does not leave it. Just like a merciful mother, providence is concerned to bring it to true loving people —— a father and mother —— who can be trusted. They help it all the days of its weakness until it matures and is able to keep itself alive on its own.

Just as this is true of man, it is true for all animals, as well as for plants and inanimate objects. They are all watched over with understanding and compassion, each sufficient to insure its own continuation and perpetuation of its species.

To one who looks at the world's economy and the factors that enter into it, there are obviously disorder and great confusions. It is as if there were no leader and no providence. Each person does as he sees fit, and seeks to destroy his friend. Wicked people attain power and the righteous crawl about without pity.

One should know that this inconsistency which we see has been felt and studied by mankind since ancient times. They had many systems to explain these two opposites which we see providence using simultaneously.

THE FIRST SYSTEM IS NATURE

This system is very ancient. These two opposites were so obvious to them, without any way to bring them together, that they (the ancients) came to the conclusion that there is a Creator who created all this. He supervises everything carefully to insure its continuation and that nothing should be lost therefrom. But this Creator lacks intelligence and feelings.

Therefore, even though he brought everything into existence and watches over everything with a wonderful wisdom, He Himself lacks knowledge. He does all of this without awareness. For if He did have knowledge and feelings, then He certainly would not permit corruption like these in the economic situation, without pity and compassion for those who suffer. They therefore call Him "Nature" as if to say a supervisor lacking knowledge and feelings. In their opinion, there is no one to complain to, or pray to. They needn't justify themselves to Him.

THE SECOND SYSTEM IS THE ONE WITH TWO POWERS

There are some who became a little wiser. It was difficult for them to accept the premise of "natural" providence. They saw that everything that exists was insured its continuation. They could not agree that the supervisor himself lacked knowledge, for nothing can give that which it does not have within itself. An idiot cannot teach his friend and make him wise. How could they say that the one who arranges wonderful things for us is not aware of what he does but does everything by chance alone. It was clear to everyone that chance cannot arrange anything with an ordered wisdom and also guarantee its continued existence forever. For this reason, they came to the second premise —— that there are two supervisors and two creators. The first created and maintains good and the second created and maintains evil. This system was widened with many proofs of this thesis.

THE THIRD SYSTEM IS THAT THERE ARE MANY G-DS

This system was born out of the bosom of the system of two powers. They divided and separated each and every action including strength, wealth, rulership, beauty, famine, death, confusion, etc. into its own class. They appointed a special creator for each one, and expanded it as they desired.

THE FOURTH SYSTEM IS THAT HE HAS STOPPED HIS ACTIVITY

In the end, as people became wiser and saw the strong connection between all the things that exist in creation, they recognized that it was absolutely impossible for there to be many gods. The question of inconsistencies in providence was raised again. They came to a new premise, viz. that in reality, the creator and supervisor over the existence of the world is wide and feeling. But because of his grandeur, He being above all evaluations, the world is, by comparison, like a mustard seed, insignificant to Him. It is not worthwhile for Him to attend to our insignificant affairs. This is the reason why our economic situation is so spoiled and everyone does as he sees fit.

Coexisting simultaneously alongside all of these systems, there were also religious systems concerning G-d's unity. Now is not the time to go into them. I just wanted to explain the origins from which all kinds of corrupted systems and surprising premises were taken. They reigned and were widespread in various times and places, as is well known.

We may conclude that the basis upon which all of the systems we spoke of were built was the opposition and contradiction between the two types of providence we feel in our world. The systems came only to heal the giant breach. The world still continues in its ways. And not only has this large, great breach not been healed, but on the contrary, it has widened before our eyes to a great chasm. We no longer see or hope for escape from it.

When I look at all these attempts that mankind has used for thousands of years to no avail, I ask whether, perhaps we should not look to the supervisor to heal the breach, but that the great connection is to be found in our very own hands.

THE NEED TO BE CAUTIOUS WITH NATURAL LAWS

We all know that mankind requires a society, that is, he cannot exist and endure without its assistance. Imagine, for example, a person who leaves society and goes to a place without other people. There he lives a life of misery and great suffering because he is unable to fill all his needs. He has no right to complain about his providence or his fate. And if he does so, that is, he complains and curses his bitter fate, then he only announces and publicizes his own stupidity. For when providence has prepared for him a restful, desireable place among society, he has no right to separate from it to a desolate place. It is forbidden to have compassion for such a person, for he goes against the nature of creation. He should live in a manner prescribed by providence. He is forsaken of pity. This sentence is accepted by all mankind without exception.

I can add to this and give reason for it from a religious perspective and judge it thusly: A creature's providence comes from the Creator. He undoubtedly has a purpose for the creature's actions, for the Creator does no action without a purpose. Therefore, anyone who transgresses any natural law which He made for us is inadvertently spoiling the purposeful goal, for the goal is undoubtedly built upon all the natural laws together. None are excluded. It is fitting for a wise worker that he should neither omit nor add even the smallest amount of work to that necessary to achieve the goal.

We find then, that when someone corrupts even a single law, his corruption insults and damages that purpose which G-d erected. Nature will therefore punish him. For this reason even we, who are G-d's creatures, are forbidden to pity the hermit. He is scorning the laws of nature and desecrating G-d's purpose.

This is the form of the sentence in my opinion. And I don't think it is worthwhile for anyone to disagree with me on the form of the sentence I have given because all sentences reduce to a single one. What is the difference, for example, if we say that the supervisor is called "Nature" that is, lacking knowledge and lacking purpose, or if we say that the supervisor is wonderfully wise, knowing, and feeling and has a purpose to his actions? In the end, we all agree that we are obliged to keep the providential, that is, the natural laws. And we all admit that anyone who transgresses the providential, i.e., the natural laws, deserves to receive whatever nature punishes him with. It is forbidden for anyone to pity him.

We see then that the nature of the sentence is the same. The only difference between the systems is one of motive. In their opinion, the sentence is obligatory, in mine, it is functional.

In order not to have to henceforth bring both forms —— nature and supervisor —— between which there is, as we have proven, no difference, it is best for us to come to a compromise. We will acccept the words of the Kabbalists who say that *Hateva* (nature) has the same numerical value as El-him (G-d). Both are equal to 86. We can now call G-d's laws natural laws and vice versa. They are the same and we shall not belabor such an insignificant point.

It is now very important for us to examine the natural laws to see what they demand of us, lest they punish us mercilessly. We have already stated that nature requires man to be a communal being. This is self-evident. But we must look at what nature obligates us to do from that aspect, that is, considering communal life.

In general we have two communal obligations. We may define them as receiving and imparting. Every member of society must receive his needs from the community. He must also work to impart to society. If he fails to fulfill these two obligations, he will be punished without pity as we have said. As for receiving, we needn't look too hard, because punishment is meted out immediately as in the example above. For this reason, there is no escape. But as for imparting to society, an individual is not punished right away, and sometimes the punishment comes indirectly. Therefore this obligation is not always fulfilled as it should be. For this reason, mankind is fried on the fire in a giant frying pan, and war, pestilence, and their consequences are still with us.

The wonder of it is that nature is like a craftsman and punishes us according to our stage of development. We see with our own eyes that as mankind develops economically, pain and suffering increase proportionately.

We now clearly see an experiential scientific basis proving that His supervision commands us to impart to others to the best of our ability. No member of society may do less than he is capable of to ensure the success and happiness of society. The lazier we are in doing this, the more nature will punish and take revenge upon us. The degree to which we suffer today added to the potential for future destruction brings us to the accurate conclusion that nature will win out in the end. We must all join hands and do what nature bids, to the degree that nature demands.

EXPERIENTIAL PROOF OF SERVING HIM

One who examines my words may claim that I have only proven that it is necessary to serve our fellow man. We have brought no practical proof of the obligation to serve G-d.

History itself has done the work for us and prepared many facts for us to see. These will suffice us to draw unmistakable conclusions. We all know that Russia is a great country with hundreds of millions of citizens. Its land resources approximate all of Europe. They also have natural resources practically unequalled in the world. They have agreed to live a communal (socialistic) existence and have practically abandoned the notion of private property. Every citizen has no concern other than for the state.

At first glance, it appears that they have acquired all the requisites for the quality of imparting to others. This is so as far as humans can discern. With all this, however, see what has happened to them. Instead of rising above and progressing beyond other bourgeois countries, they have gone steadily downward. Not only are they unable to raise the quality of life for their workers more than bourgeois countries, but they cannot even guarantee them bread or clothing.

In truth, this fact is quite astonishing. Based on the riches of the country and its large population, it should not have, according to human calculation, reached this condition. But this nation (Russia) has sinned a great sin and G-d will not forgive them. This precious work of imparting to others which they began to implement, must be done for heaven's sake, not for mankind's sake. Because they don't work for His sake, they don't merit to be sustained by natural law.

Imagine to yourself if every Russian were cautious to fulfill the commandment of "Thou shalt love the L-rd thy G-d with all thy heart and all thy soul and all that He hath given thee" (Deut.). Imagine also that he concerned himself to fill the needs and requirements of his friends, to the same degree he was naturally concerned for his own needs. As it is written, "Love thy friend as thyself" (Lev.). Imagine also that G-d Himself was the goal of each citizen. That is, that the citizen, as he was working for the sake of the community, also hoped to merit to cleave to G-d as a result of his labor. He hoped to reach the root of all truth, all good and all pleasant things.

Surely there would be no doubt that in a matter of just a few years Russia would be richer than all countries in the world put together. For then they would be able to take advantage of all the natural resources in their rich country. They would be an example for all other countries and would be called "blessed by G-d".

However, when all work of imparting to others is based solely on communal welfare, then the foundation is shaky. For who or what forces the individual to work and weary himself for the community's sake? One can never expect a dry lifeless principle to supply "motive power" (motivation) to developed people, to say nothing of undeveloped people.

The question becomes one of from where the worker or farmer will find the motive power sufficient to get him to work? Giving him his daily bread is insufficient motivation for him to exert himself when no goal or additional rewards can be attained

It is well known to natural scientists that an unmotivated person will not make even the slightest movements unless he sees in it some personal improvement. For example, if a person takes his hand off a chair and puts it on a table, it is because he thinks that he will benefit from doing so. If he didn't think so, he would leave his hand on the chair all his life. He would never move it, let alone do something requiring a great effort.

If you might suggest that we appoint taskmasters over him in a manner that anyone who is lazy will be punished, and his daily wages reduced accordingly, then I will ask another question. From where will the supervisors themselves draw the motive power for their work? They must stand in a special place and supervise people who must work and weary themselves. This too is a great effort, perhaps even greater than that of the workers.

The whole situation is similar to trying to run a machine without giving it fuel. They must fail because the natural laws will punish them. They are incapable of keeping nature's commands of imparting to others in the same manner as if they were serving G-d. In the latter case, they cleave to Him (as explained in chap. 1, par. 6). As a result of this cleaving, the worker receives a proportional amount of his pleasant influence. It grows to the degree that he recognizes G-d's truth and it develops until he merits the great distinction of knowing G-d as the Bible says, "the eye hath not seen another G-d but Thee." (Isaiah, 64:3).

Imagine! If the farmer and the worker perceived this goal as they worked for the community's welfare, then for certain they would not need supervisors standing over them. They would already have motive power sufficient for a great effort. They could raise the community to the heights of accomplishment.

To reach this degree of understanding requires much effort and must be done in an orderly fashion. But all can see that they (Russia) do not merit existence without it. Nature is very stubborn and knows no compromise.

The examples used are based upon practical experience taken from contemporary historical events. I have clearly proven that there is absolutely no remedy for mankind. They must accept upon themselves the commandment of providence to impart to others in order to do G-d's will. They must do so in accordance with two Biblical passages:

The first passage is, "Love thy friend as thyself." This passage explains the degree to which one must exert himself in imparting to others for the good of the community. It must be no less than one would naturally exert himself to fill his own needs. Not only this, but one must place the needs of others before his very own, (Chapter 1, par. 4).

The second passage is, "And thou shalt love the L-rd thy G-d with all thy heart and all thy soul and all that He hath given thee." This is the goal that one should bear in mind when he is working for the communal good. He must feel that he is doing his work solely to find grace in G-d's eyes.

The Bible says, "If you agree and listen, you shall eat from the finest of the land" (Is. 1:19). All poverty and affliction will vanish and everyone's happiness will increase beyond measure. But if we refuse and don't want to enter into agreement to serve G-d as described above, then nature and its laws stand ready to take revenge upon us. She will not ease up on us, as we proved above. In the end she will be victorious and we will receive all the bitterness she decrees upon us.

I have now given you a scientific practical study based upon knowledgeable, practical criticism pertaining to the absolute obligation for all creatures to accept upon themselves the service of G-d with all their hearts and all their souls and all that G-d has given them.

AN EXPLANATION OF THE MISHNAH, "EVERYTHING IS GIVEN WITH A PLEDGE AND A NET IS SPREAD OUT OVER ALL LIVING CREATURES" (ABOT: 3, 17)

Now that we know all that has been said above, we can

understand a difficult Mishnah (Rabbinical teaching):

> R. Akiba used to say, "Everything is given with a pledge and a net is spread out over all living creatures. The store is open, the storekeeper extends credit, the ledger is open and the hand is writing. Anyone wishing to, may come and borrow. The collectors come around everyday and exact from a person whether he knows it or not. They have something to rely on. The judgement is truthful and everything is prepared for the feast."

There is good reason why this Mishnah remains closed without any hint of its interpretation. It shows that it is very deep. But it is very well explained based on the ideas we have acquired until now.

THE WHEEL OF CHANGING FORM

I begin with the words of our Sages regarding the chain of generations in the world. They say that although we see the physical bodies changing from generation to generation, this applies only to the body. The souls, which are the essence of the body, are not subject to change. Rather they migrate and inhabit body after body in generation after generation. Those very same souls that were present in the generation of the flood (Noah), returned again in the generation of upheaval (Tower of Babel), and then during the Egyptian exile, and again with the Egyptian exodus, etc. This process continues to our generation and will continue until the world is complete. It proceeds in a manner that we have no new souls as we have new bodies in our world. There are a fixed number of souls which reincarnate into new shapes. That is, each time, they are enclothed in a new body in a generation.

When we calculate generations according to souls, each generation is calculated from the beginning of creation until the completion of the world. One generation may last several thousand years until it has developed sufficiently and arrived at its own completion. It is unimportant that, in the meantime, each and every soul has changed its body thousands of times. The soul, which is the essence of the body, does not suffer in the process.

There are many proofs for this and a special body of knowledge called the secret of soul reincarnation. Now is not the time to explain it. But for the sake of completion and for those who are not familiar with it, it is worthwhile to point out that reincarnation also applies to everything in our physical world. Each and every thing lives eternally. Even though we see that everything that exists eventually dies, this is just external appearance. In truth, reincarnation occurs. Nothing rests or remains quiet for even an instant. Instead, it reincarnates into another form without losing anything in the process. Physicists have expaned on this principle.

We now come to the explanation of the Mishnah. It says, "everything is given with a pledge." This is similar to someone who lends his friend a sum of money in order that he (the lender) should be a partner with him (the borrower) in the profit. In order that the lender be certain that he will not lose his money, he takes collateral. In this way, he is not concerned over his money. The same is true of the creation of the world and its continuing existence. G-d created men to work it and to ultimately achieve cleaving to him (See chapter 1, par. 6). So we must consider who it is who will force mankind to do G-d's work until they arrive at their final goal. Therefore it says, "everything is given with a pledge." Nothing that G-d gave mankind as part of creation was given without preconditions. Rather, G-d insured Himself with a pledge.

What kind of pledge did G-d take? The Mishnah answers, "a net is spread out over all living things." G-d was smart (so to speak). He spread a giant net over all mankind which no one can escape. All mankind must get caught in this net, and must accept upon themselves G-d's service until they reach their goal. This is the pledge that G-d insured Himself with in order that He not be fooled by man.

The Mishnah next explains the specifics. "The store is open." That is, the world appears to be wide open and without owners. Everyone can come in and take whatever he wants for free. But, Rabbi Akiba warns us, "the storekeeper extends credit." Even though you don't see a storekeeper there, you should know that there is one. The reason he doesn't get paid now is that he is giving it to you on credit.

And how does he know what your bill is? To this the Mishnah answers, "the record is open and the hand is writing." There is a general ledger and in it each and every act is written down. Nothing is lost. The reference is to the natural laws of development which G-d established, which continually push us onward. This means that the corruptions of mankind are themselves the cause and creation of all good situations. Every good situation is nothing more than the fruit borne by a bad situation which preceeded it.(*see further in text for explanation).

Therefore, the values of good or bad are not relative to the situation itself, but must be taken for a more general perspective. Every situation which brings mankind closer to the goal of cleaving to G-d is good, and every situation which does the opposite, is bad.

The laws of development are based upon these values. Corruption and evil that are present in a situation are merely a cause for the good situation to follow. The time that any situation exists is only that time necessary for the evil to grow so great that the public cannot stand it any longer. Then they will unite to destroy it, create a better situation, and reform the generation.

The new situation exists long enough for the sparks of evil contained within it (the new order) to ripen and grow unbearable. At that time, it, too, will be destroyed and a more comfortable situation established in its place. In this manner, the situations are clarified one after the other, step by step, until they are completely rectified of all evil.

We now see that the seeds from which all good situations grow are none other than the corruptions themselves. Each and every evil perpetrated by wrongdoers of a generation combine until the community can no longer endure it. They (society) then arise, destroy the evil, and create a more desirable situation. Evil, in all its aspects, is nothing more than a driving force for the development of a better situation.

Rabbi Akiba, in our Mishnah, said, "the ledger is open and the hand is writing." Every situation that a generation encounters is like a ledger. It accumulates to an intolerable degree and society then destroys it, establishing a more desirable order. We see that each and every action is accounted for in the ledger, as we have said.

The Mishnah continues, "anyone who wishes to, may come and borrow." The reference is to anyone who believes that the world is not a wide open, ownerless store. Rather, he believes that in the world to come there is a shopkeeper who collects his full due from everyone who takes anything. Such a person strives to reach the goal of creation during the time that he is dependent on the said store. This person is considered one who desires to borrow. Even before he extends his hand to take something from this world (the store), he knows that he is taking it on loan and must pay its price. He accepts upon himself to work towards the goal while he is dependent on the store. In this way, he guarantees that he will pay his debt by reaching the goal (of cleaving to G-d). He is therefore called a borrower because he obligates himself to repay.

Rabbi Akiba describes for us two types of people. The first type think that the world is an open store without an owner. Referring to them he says, "the ledger is open and the hand is writing." In spite of the fact that they don't see the account, their actions are recorded in the book. The natural laws of development apply to them and the deeds of these people lead to good outcomes in the manner discussed above.

The second type is called "one who wishes to borrow." They take account of the owner. Whenever they take something from the store, they take it as a loan. They promise the shopkeeper that they will pay the determined price of using the item to reach the desired goal. Of them, Rabbi Akiba says, "anyone who wishes to borrow may come and do so."

What is the difference between the two types? In the first instance, the goal is forced upon him via the laws of development. In the second, the goal is attained by submitting oneself to serving G-d. Both cases have the same final outcome.

Rabbi Akiba answers and says, "the collectors come around

every day and collect from a person whether he knows it or not." It's true that both of them pay the same price daily. The positive forces that appear when one does G-d's service become trustworthy collectors and collect the precise amount due, on a daily basis, until the full amount has been collected. In exactly the same way, the steadfast forces of the law of development become collectors and do the same thing.

There is a major difference between them. This is what Rabbi Akiba means when he says, "whether he knows it or not." When the debt is collected by the development's collectors, they collect without man being aware of it. The forces of debt act strongly and push a person from behind, forcing mankind to take a step forward. The debts are collected against one's will and take the form of suffering.

The second type of people pay their debt themselves by serving G-d. They perform the specific services which hasten development of the sense of recognizing evil (see chapter 2, Development With and Without Knowing It). As a result of this service, we profit in two ways. First, the forces which are revealed through serving G-d pull us, almost magnetically, from in front. We are hurriedly drawn to them in a spirit of love and desire. They have no associated pain and suffering as the first way. Secondly, they speed us to the desired goal. These people are the righteous and the prophets of every generation who attain the goal. (See chapter 3, Axis of Kabbalah).

We see that there is a great difference between those who pay knowingly and those who pay unknowingly. The difference is like comfortable pleasant light compared to darkness filled with suffering and pain.

Rabbi Akiba continues, "they have something to rely on and

the judgement is true." Those who pay back on their own "have something to rely on." Performing his service unleashes great powers to bring us to the desired goal, and it is worthwhile for them to submit themselves to his yoke.

To those who repay without knowing it, he says, "the judgement is true." At first glance, we might be surprised at His supervision, that He allows all the corruption and suffering that burn men alive without mercy. Therefore he says, "the judgement is true."

"Everything is prepared for the feast," that is for the true goal and the supernal pleasure which is destined to be revealed. All the toil and weariness and suffering that afflict the various generations and eras are similar to the host who works hard to prepare a banquet for his invited guests. He constantly keeps in mind his goal of seeing his guests sitting happily around the table. He knows this must ultimately occur. Therefore, Rabbi Akiba says, "the judgement is true and everything is prepared for the feast."

The same idea is expressed in the Midrash (Genesis Rabbah, chapter 8) referring to creation of the world.

The angels asked G-d, "What is man that you are mindful of him, and the son of man that you think of him?" (Ps. 8:5). Why do you need this trouble? G-d said to them, 'sheep and oxen' (Ps. 8:6) why were they created?... It is like a king who had a castle filled with all good things but he had no guests. What pleassure did he get from filling it?" The angels said to Him, "G-d, our master, how great is Your Name in the world." (Ps. 8:10).

The angels foresaw all pain and suffering that was to ultimately befall mankind. They were surprised and asked what purpose all this trouble served. G-d answered that He had a castle filled with all good things and He had no guests to invite other than mankind. The angels weighed the pleasures that lay waiting for the guests against the suffering and troubles that were destined to reach mankind. When they saw that it was worthwhile for mankind to suffer in order to reach the good that was waiting for it, they agreed to the creation of man.

This is precisely what Rabbi Akiba said, "the judgement is true and everything is prepared for the feast." Even before creation all the creatures were registered as invited guests. G-d's plan made it incumbent on all of them to attend the banquet, whether they know it or not.

The prophet Isaiah, in his prophecy of peace said, "And the wolf shall dwell with the lamb, and the leopard shall lie down with the kid" (Isaiah 11:6). The reason he gives for this is, "for the earth shall be full of knowledge of the Lord, as the waters cover the sea." (ibid; 11:9). The prophet hangs worldly peace on the world being full of knowledge of G-d.

This is precisely what we said above. The egoistic opposition between people and along with it, the ever-sharpening international tensions will not disappear through any human strategem, whatever it may be. We see with our own eyes how the unfortunate sick world tosses and turns in pain without relief on any side. Mankind has already gone to the extreme right as in Germany, or to the extreme left as in Russia. Not only have they not made it easier on themselves, but they have become sicker and in greater pain. The cries reach heaven.

We see that they have no other choice than to accept His yoke and to know Him. They must direct all their actions to filling His will and reaching His goal. This is what He had in mind for them before creation. And when they do this, it is obvious to all that all remnants of hatred and jealousy will vanish from the earth. All mankind will be united into a single body with a single mind, filled with knowledge of G-d. So world peace and knowledge of G-d are, as we can see, equivalent.

Right after this the prophet (Isaiah) says, "And on that day, the L-rd will set His hand again a second time to recover the remnant of His people... and gather together the scattered of Judah from the four corners of the earth." (Is. 11:11,12). We conclude that worldly peace is a preliminary to the gathering of the exiles.

With this we can understand what our Sages said, (TB, Uktzin end) "the L-rd did not find any vessel (capable of) sustaining blessing for Israel except for peace, as it is written, 'G-d will give might to His nation, G-d will bless His nation with peace.'"

At first glance, we are surprised at the rhetoric "a vessel capable of sustaining blessing for Israel." Furthermore, how do they deduce this from the given sentence? The sentence is explained exactly as we did Isaiah's prophecy. World peace must precede the gathering of the exiles. Therefore, the sentence says, "G-d will give His nation might," meaning that in the future, when G-d gives might that is everlasting revival to His nation, then "G-d will bless His nation with peace." He will first bless His nation of Israel with worldly peace and then He will redeem the remnant of His people.

This is the explanation our Sages gave for the sentence. The blessing of worldly peace precedes might, that is, redemption. For "G-d did not find any vessel capable of sustaining blessing for Israel except for peace." That is, as long as egoism and self-love prevail in the world, then Israel will be unable to purely serve G-d in imparting to others. (See explanation on the sentence "And you will be unto me a nation of priests" in the second chapter).

Experience has shown us the same thing. Returning to Israel and rebuilding the Holy Temple (in the period of Ezra and Nehemiah) were unable to take hold and bring the blessings which G-d promised our forefathers.

Our Sages said, "G-d did not find..." That is, until now, the Israelites have had no vessel of sustaining the blessing G-d had made to our forefathers. The promise that we inherit the land of Israel forever has not yet come about, because world peace is the only vessel that can enable us to receive the blessing of our forefathers. Such is the prophecy of Isaiah.

CHAPTER 8

FREE WILL

The Mishnah says that Rabbi Jose b. Kisma was asked by a man to dwell in the man's town. In return he would receive a thousand golden dinars. Rabbi Jose b. Kisma answered "even if you give me all the silver and gold and precious stones and pearls in the world, I will live only in a place of Torah" (Abot 6:9). It is hard for us to comprehend how he could pass up millions of gold dinars for such a small thing like not wanting to live in a town that did not house Torah scholars. After all, he himself was very wise and had no need of someone to learn Torah from.

Actually, it is very simple based on what we have been saying. It is something which we should all be aware of. We have said that everyone has a personality. (* The word personality as used here refers to the natural instincts and tendencies that are part of a person). But the potentials become manifest only in conjunction with the immediate environment. It is similar to wheat which is planted in the ground. The potential is not realized without the right soil, rain and sunlight which make up the environment.

Rabbi Jose b. Kisma figured correctly. If he left the good environment that he was in and went to a bad, debased city, devoid of Torah, then not only would he become confused in what he already knew, but also the rest of the potential buried in his personality and not yet realized would remain hidden. They would no longer have an appropriate environment to bring them out. This is what we explained above that the ability of a person to control himself is relative to his surroundings. These factors must be accounted for when considering reward and punishment.

Now it is not surprising that Rabbi Jose b. Kisma chose good and forsook evil. He was not tempted by physical possessions. As the Mishnah continues, "when a person dies, silver, gold, precious stones and pearls do not accompany him, but only Torah and good deeds" (ibid). Similarly, our Sages have warned us, "Make for yourself a Rabbi and buy yourself a friend." (Abot, 1:6). Other books say the same things. Only by his choice of environment are benefit or discredit determined. But once he has chosen his environment, then he is in its hands, like clay in the hands of a potter.

Some modern secular scholars, upon reflection on the matter under discussion saw that a person's thoughts are like fruits that sprout from life's experiences. They concluded that the mind has absolutely no control over the body. Daily occurrences leave their impression on the mind and they control a person. A person's mind is like a mirror that receives the forms of the objects before it. And while the mirror holds these images before it, it is unable to move the images at all.

In their opinion, the same is true of the mind. Despite the fact that the mind is aware of all occurrences in life, and their cause and effect relationship, the mind itself does not control the body at all. It is unable to bring about motion to draw the body to beneficial things and keep it away from danger.

They view the spiritual and the physical as very far from one another. Nothing can reconcile the difference between them in a way to allow the spiritual mind to operate in and move a physical body.

Their very sharpness, however, is their own downfall. A person's imagination works in his mind the same way that a microscope aids the eyes. Without a microscope, one is unable to see anything dangerous because it is too small. But once he is able to see it with the microscope, man can avoid it. So the microscope, not the senses, brings a person to avoidance of danger. The senses were unaware of the danger.

In exactly this way the mind controls a person's body to keep him from danger, and lead him to good. Whenever one of the faculties of the body is too weak to recognize if it will be benefitted or hurt by something, then a person need only rely on his mind. Not only this, but because a person recognizes that the mind can deduce conclusions from life experiences, he is capable of accepting the opinion of a trusted friend. He does this even though he himself has not experienced the concept. For example, when a person asks a doctor for an opinion, he accepts it and carries it out even though he himself does not understand it.

We see that a person uses the minds of other people and in so doing is helped no less than by using his own mind. Compare this with what was said in chapter 4 (Quality of Religion). We said that there are two ways that providence guarantees that a person will achieve the desired goal: the way of suffering and the way of Torah. The clarity in the path we described as the way of Torah, stems from those insights which were revealed and passed on in a long unbroken chain by the prophets and renowned people. A person can come today and take advantage of their (the prophets') insight. He benefits from them just as he does from the things he experiences in his own life. It is clear then that a person is relieved of having to go through all the bitter experiences of life until he develops his own clarity of mind. He doesn't suffer and he gains time.

We can compare this to a person who refuses to follow a doctor's advice until he understands for himself how the advice will help cure him. So he begins to learn medicine. He could die before he understands it well enough.

The same is true of the way of suffering compared to the way of Torah. One who doesn't believe in the insights that the Torah advises us to accept on faith must arrive on his own to the same conclusions. He can only do this by the chain of cause and effect in daily life. The latter are powerful experiences capable of developing within him a stage of recognizing evil. This is accomplished as we have explained, without his knowledge. Only as a by-product of his attempt to achieve a good environment is he brought to understand these things.

The topic of how a man recognizes the state of his environment and how he goes from one situation to the next will be explained in the following chapter.

INDIVIDUAL FREEDOM

We can now properly understand the idea of individual freedom. It refers only to one's personality, that is, to all the tendencies that a person inherits from his ancestors. They are a primitive quality in a person and it is only through them that one person differs from another. We may see a thousand people in the same surroundings. Even the last three things they experienced may be identical. Still, no two of them will have the identical character. This is true because each of them has his own unique personality. It is similar to the instinct in wheat. Despite the fact that the last three events have influenced it, it still retains the former character of wheat. It can never change to another species.

This is the general rule: every situation is the result of causes which precede it and it changes with successive events. Even if the three most recent occurrences cause a major change in the situation, its general underlying appearance remains. A person, for example, can never change his character to that of another person, just as barley can never become wheat.

We see that each and every personality is the sum total of the expression of the many traits which it consists of. Therefore, no two people will have identical characters. The personality is the true inheritance of an individual and it is forbidden for anyone to damage or change it. It is the destiny of each of the traits in one's personality to express itself and mature. As the indivudal matures, the trait matures.

Due to the law of development which constantly pushes him forward in the scenario described, we see that each and every tendency must, in the end, become enlightened to a very great degree. Anyone who destroys another's tendencies causes the trait that is to finally emerge to be lost from the world. No one else besides that individual will ever again manifest that trait.

We must also understand that once a trait matures and becomes enlightened, then we no longer recognize in it good or evil. These differences exist only in the immature stage. Not even the slightest amount of good or evil remains in them upon maturity. We will expand on this in future chapters.

(*Translator's note: We have not meritted to receive these chapters).

Now we understand the magnitude of the iniquity done by those nations which embitter their minorities and strip them of their freedom, not allowing them to carry on the customs they inherited from their ancestors. They are doing the equivalent of murder. Even those irreligious people who don't believe in Divine providence can understand the obligation to insure an individual's freedom. Natural law obligates this.

We see with our own eyes how the downfall of all nations throughout history came about solely because of oppression of minorities and individuals. The latter eventually overcame and destroyed their oppressors.

It is now clear to everyone that worldly peace cannot be established if we do not consider the freedom of the individual. Without it, there can be no lasting peace.

Thus far we have precisely defined the individual as a function of how society nurtures him. Yet, a question remains —— where is the individual himself? All that we have said regarding the individual concerns itself with what he inherits from his ancestors. Where is the individual, the inheritor who receives all this? From what has been said until now, we have not found the separate entity we can define as the "self."

Also, of what consequence is the single cause (we will use the term initial cause) which is the long chain of people in generation after generation which determined the inherited image of the individual? And of what consequence are the last three causes (we will use the term secondary causes; see beginning of this chapter), which are the thousands of people in the contemporaneous society.

In the end, a person is like a societal machine. He is passive to two types of communities. From the perspective of the initial cause, he is passive to the previous generations and from the secondary causes, he is passive relative to his contemporaries.

This is a perpetual question and for this reason many people oppose this naturalistic explanation, even though they agree that it has merit. These people instead choose mataphysical, dualistic or trancendental systems to describe some spiritual essence called a "soul" dwelling in the body. The soul is what enlightens and operates the body. IT is the essence of the person, the "self."

The intent of these systems is to ease the mind. Their shortcoming is that they have no scientific explanation of how a spiritual entity can have any contact with physical atoms, that is, with the body. How can it cause any motion? All their wisdom and delving has not helped them to bridge the gap between the spiritual soul and the physical atom. Science has not benefitted at all from all these metaphysical systems.

In order to take a step forward in science, we need only the Kabbalah. All the world's wisdoms are included in Kabbalah. (We have explained this in Panim Masbirot on Etz Chaim, Chapter 1). It is explained in terms of the lights and vessels found in all the upper worlds. When G-d created the world, he created in EX NIHILO (out of nothing). The essence of this great creation is totally defined within the framework of the "Desire to Receive." Nothing in anything else that was created is new. The rest is not considered creation EX NIHILO. All else stems directly from His essence just as the light comes from the sun. Nothing new is created in the light. It is merely the substance of the sun emanating therefrom in an altered form.

This is not the case with the "Desire to Receive." Prior to creation, the Desire to Receive did not exist. It was not part of G-d for He preceeded everything, so from whom could He receive? So this Desire to Receive is what G-d created EX NIHILO. Nothing else is new and therefore we cannot say that it was created. Therefore, all the vessels and bodies in the spiritual and physical worlds contain within them an aspect of the Desire to Receive.

The Desire to Receive has within it two potentials, called the drawing (or pulling) force and the pushing force. The reason for this is that every vessel or body having a Desire to Receive is limited to the quantity and quality of what it can receive. But because the limitations are external, they are unnatural and undesirable. In this way, the Desire to Receive, although it literally implies a drawing or pulling force, also contains an aspect of undesirability. This must be well understood.

The Kabbalah does not speak at all of our physical world. Yet all the worlds obey the same laws (see Chapter 3). Therefore, we can say that all the physical things of our universe, whether human, animal, plant, or inanimate, physical or spiritual are unique. If we examine down to the most minute aspect by which one object differs from another, we find that all the differences reduce to the Desire to Receive. It is the Desire to Receive that gives it its form and constitution, both quantitatively and qualitatively. The Desire to Receive renews it and forces it to grow. The Desire to Receive is the source of both the pulling and pushing force.

The Desire to Receive has more than just the two forces we discussed. It controls the influence which flows directly from G-d. The influence flows equally for all creation, and, being direct from G-d, cannot be considered as something created EX NIHILO. The influence is not a function of the indivudal but applies to all creation, large and small, each according to its Desire to Receive. In this way, the Desire to Receive defines the difference between each and every creature.

I have now clearly proven the existence of the "self" (ego) of every individual as being the Desire to Receive. Even secular scientists with their mentalist or automotan models must accept it. And now we no longer need all the other metaphysical systems either. It obviously makes no difference if this force called the Desire to Receive is a function of the material and brought about by chemical reactions, or if the reverse is true. The important thing is to recognize that the force is present in every creature and every atom. And the Desire to Receive is the single property by which one thing differs from all others in its virginity. This applies to single atoms and to the entire group of atoms that constitute the body.

All other aspects of the Desire to Receive have no relationship to the uniqueness of the object and to its "self" except through the influence which flows equally to all of them from G-d. These other aspects have nothing to do with the physical entities themselves.

Now we will elaborate further on how what we called personality affects an individual's freedom of choice. All a person's ancestors have left their influence on the personality. As explained above, the word "self" refers to the Desire to Receive as it manifests, with all its limitations, connections and individual characters.

We see then, that all the tendencies that a person inherits from his ancestors are only the boundaries that define his Desire to Receive. These include what he is attracted to and what repels him. They manifest as tendencies to be cheap or frivolous, social or asocial, etc. They constitute the "self" of an individual and it is they who strive to keep him alive. Therefore, if we destroy any tendency from an individual, then we are cutting off one of the limbs of his "self." This is a great loss to all of creation for these tendencies will never appear again anywhere else in the world.

Having clearly proven that an individual has freedom of choice based on natural laws, we will next examine to what degree he may exercise it without infringing on moral or political laws. Primarily, we will consider how it applies to our holy Torah.

The Bible says (Ex. 23:2) "(one should) follow the majority." That is, whenever there is a dispute between an individual and a group, we must decide according to the needs of the many. We see then that the group has the authority to suspend the rights of the individual.

Here we have an even more serious question. This law appears to cause mankind to regress, instead of progress. If the majority of mankind are not advanced, the advanced will always constitute the majority. If we always follow the majority opinion then the opinions and needs of the wiser, more advanced people will never be enacted. This seals the fate of mankind to regress for they cannot take even a small step forward.

The answer is to be found in what we explained in Chapter 4 concerning the obligation to observe the natural laws. Providence (G-d) has commanded us to live as the Torah prescribes. We must therefore do everything necessary for the continuation of society. If we are even a bit lenient, then nature will take its revenge, and it will follow nature's rules. It doesn't matter if we understand the rules or not.

We see with our own eyes that life in society must be according to the law of following the majority. This law can settle arguments and disagreements in society. It is this law alone that permits society to continue. For this reason it is considered one of the natural laws of providence. We must accept it and observe it cautiously without trying to understand or rationalize it. It is similar to other laws in the Torah which are natural laws and come to us from above down.

In Chapter 3 we said that all the natural laws are only because they derive from the laws that apply to the upper worlds. The stubbornness we see in nature exists because it has a counterpart in the upper spiritual worlds. With this in mind, we can understand that all the commandments of the Torah are no more than the laws that apply in the upper worlds which are the roots of all the natural laws in our world.

For this reason, the laws of the Torah are as identical to natural laws as two drops of water. And the law of following the majority opinion is a natural law as well as a Torah law. In spite of this, the question of regressing has not been answered, but remains our concern.

Providence, however, is not concerned about this regression. It has already covered mankind on two ways, viza the way of Torah and the way of punishment. Providence is certain that mankind will constantly develop and advance toward the goal. It is not at all concerned. We previously explained this when we discussed the Mishnah which says that everything is given with a pledge.

CHAPTER 9

ON CONCLUSION OF THE ZOHAR

It is well known that the purpose of engaging in Torah and *mitzvot* is to cleave to G-d, as it is written, "and to cleave unto Him" (Dt. 11:22). We must understand what is meant by cleaving. After all, our minds cannot fathom Him at all.

Our Sages have previously asked this same question concerning "and to cleave unto Him." They asked how it is possible to cleave unto Him, for, He is a consuming fire. They answered that one should cleave to His attributes. Just as He is merciful, we too should be merciful; just as He is compassionate, we, too, should be compassionate, etc.

It appears difficult to understand how the Sages did not stick to the literal meaning. The Bible clearly says, "and to cleave unto HIM." If the interpretation were to cleave to His attributes then the Bible should have said "and to cleave to His ways." Why does it say "and to cleave unto HIM?"

The answer has to do with how closeness is determined. In the physical world, we determine cleaving by spatial proximity. Separation is understood as spatial distance. But in the spiritual plane where space does not apply, cleavage and separation are not determined by spatial relationships. In the spiritual realm, the degree to which two things are similar is the measure of cleaving and the degree of dissimilarity is the measure of separation. Just as an axe cuts and splits something physical in two by separating the two parts from one another, so a difference in form separates something spiritual into two parts. If the difference between them is small, we say the distance between them is small, and if the difference is great, we say they are far from one another. If they are of opposite form, we say they are at opposite poles.

Take, for example, two people who hate one another. We say that they are as far apart as east and west. And if they love one another, then we say they are of one flesh. Here we are not speaking of spatial proximity or distance, instead we refer to similarity of form (feelings). When two people love one another, we say their forms are similar. Each loves what the other loves and hates what the other hates. As a result they (are close to) (cleave to) and love one another. But if there are differences in form, that is, if one loves something in spite of the fact that the other hates it, then they will hate one another proportional to the degree of their differences. And if they are opposites and each loves what the other hates, then they are as far apart as east and west.

We see then that a difference in form separates in the spiritual realm, just as an axe does in a physical realm. Furthermore, the degree of separation depends on the degree of dissimilarity between them and the measure of closeness depends on the measure of similarity.

Now we see how right our Sages were when they explained "and to cleave to Him" as cleaving to His characteristics, "just as He is etc." They did not change the literal meaning, but rather explained it in its most literal sense, for spiritual closeness is only attained by similarity of form. As a result of our imitating G-d's attributes, we are cleaving to Him. This is the meaning of "just as He is merciful, etc." All of G-d's actions are to impart to and help others and not for His own sake. He, of course, lacks nothing, and besides, from whom shall He receive? In the same way, all of our actions must be to impart to and help others and in this manner, we will be similar to Him and attain spiritual cleaving.

In imitating G-d, there are two aspects, relating to the mind and heart respectively. When we observe the Torah and the commandments for G-d's sake, then we are imitating G-d from the mind aspect. G-d does not ponder whether or not He exists or whether or not He supervises His creation, etc., so it is forbidden for anyone who wishes to imitate Him to think of these things. Clearly G-d does not think of them, and there can be no greater dissimilarity than this. Therefore, anyone who thinks these things is very far from Him. Such a person will never be able to imitate Him. On this our Sages have said "everything you do should be for Heaven's sake." (Abot 2:12, Zohar, 3:516). One should do nothing which does not bring about cleaving to G-d. Everything one does should be to impart and to help other people. Then one will be imitating Him and cleaving to Him completely.

One may ask how it is possible that everything a person does should be for the benefit of others? After all, he must work to sustain himself and his family. The answer is that anything that he is forced to do to keep himself alive is neither positive nor negative and doesn't count as something he is doing solely for himself.

It will amaze anyone who studies this deeply how it is possible for someone to completely imitate G-d. How can every act one does be to impart to others when the very essence of a person is the Desire to Receive (see previous chapter)? Furthermore, it is only natural that when a person does something to benefit another that he should expect some kind of reward. And if he is unsure about a reward, then he will not perform the act. How is it possible that everything he does will be to impart to others and he will not work to help himself?

I admit that this is something very difficult to do. A person does not have the ability to change his nature, that is, his Desire to Receive. Certainly he can't go from one extreme to the other, taking nothing for himself and only imparting to others. For this reason, G-d gave us the Torah and *mitzvot.* We are commanded to observe them for G-d's sake. Through observing the Torah and *mitzvot* for Heaven's sake, and not for our own benefit, we are able to reverse our nature. There is no other way. But, if a person observes the Torah and *mitzvot* for his own benefit and not for G-d's sake, then not only will his Desire to Receive not be reversed, but, on the contrary, it will increase over its natural endowment. (This has been explained in the Introduction to the Sulam commentary on the Zohar, first volume, pars. 30,31).

What can be said of a person who merits to cleave to G-d? There are no explicit answers given anywhere, only hints. For the sake of completion of this chapter, I will explain using an example.

The body with all its limbs forms a single entity. The brain can switch its concentration to each limb as needed. If the brain thinks that it can benefit from the action of a particular limb, then that limb is made aware of this and acts accordingly. If any limb is uncomfortable, the brain is immediately aware of it and moves it to a more comfortable position. But, if a particular limb were removed from the body, then the two (body and limb) become separate entitites and the brain is no longer aware of the needs of that removed limb. The limb is also unaware of what the brain is thinking and cannot follow its commands. If a doctor were to come and reconnect the limb as it had been before, then each becomes once again aware of the other.

The qualities of a person who cleaves to G-d is understood by means of the above example. In my Introduction to the Zohar (vol. I, par. 9, and Idra Zota), I proved that the soul is a light that emanates directly from G-d. It differs from G-d in that it has a Desire to Receive. The latter was placed there because G-d wanted mankind to receive pleasure. This difference, represented by the Desire to Receive, separates the light (soul) from G-d and makes it a separate entity. The reader is referred to the above sources.

What comes out of this is that prior to creation, every soul was a part of G-d's essence. At the time of creation when the Desire to Receive was added, it attained a new form and became separate from G-d, for G-d's nature is solely to impart.

The soul now completely resembles the limb, which was removed from the body. Prior to the separation, when the body was a single entity, the two had been one and communicated with one another. After the limb is removed and they become separate entitites, they no longer communicate.

Add to this the fact that the soul is enclothed in a body in this world and we see that all the ties it originally had with G-d are severed and they are two separate entities.

The qualities of a person who merits to once again cleave to G-d are now self-evident. When a person, through the power of performing the Torah and *mitzvot*, transforms his Desire to Receive into a desire to impart, and all his actions are solely to impart and benefit his fellow man, then he is imitating his Creator. Such a person is exactly like a severed limb that has been reattached and once again communicates with the body. The soul when it exactly imitates its Creator, once again knows the thoughts of the Creator as it had prior to separation. On this the Bible says, "know the G-d of thy fathers." (1 ch. 18:9). The soul merits a complete, G-d-like knowledge. It knows all the secets of the Torah, for the latter are the thoughts of G-d.

Rabbi Meir said, "Anyone who learns Torah for its own sake merits many things. The secrets of the Torah are revealed to him... and he becomes like a fountain that gains vigor.... (Abot 6:1). Compare this with what we have said. When one practices Torah for its own sake, and his intention is to create pleasure for G-d and not to benefit himself, he is guaranteed of cleaving to G-d. When all his actions are solely to benefit others and not for his own sake, then he is exactly like G-d, whose very action is for the benefit of others. In this way, a person's soul cleaves to G-d, just as it had prior to creation. Such a person merits many things including the secrets of the Torah. Once he reunites with G-d, he knows His thoughts, just like the reattached limb. G-d's thoughts are, as we have said, called the secrets of the Torah.

We see then, that a person who learns Torah for its own sake merits learning the secrets of the Torah. He becomes like a gushing fountain as the partitions that separated him from G-d are removed and he becomes one with G-d, just as he was prior to creation.

In truth, all the Torah in both its revealed and hidden aspects are G-d's thoughts. It resembles a person who is drowning in a river. His friend throws him a rope to save him. If the drowning man holds onto the rope, his friend can save him and pull him out of the river. The Torah, which is G-d's thoughts, is the rope that G-d has thrown to mankind to save them from the klippot (veils or husks that prevent G-d's light and influence from shining upon us). That part of the rope that is near mankind is the revealed portion of the Torah. It requires no special meditations or thoughts. Furthermore, even if a person has undesirable thoughts when he performs a *mitzvah* G-d still accepts it. As our Sages said, "A person should always observe the Torah and *mitzvot* even not for its own sake for he will eventually come to observe it for its own sake." (TV Pesachim, 506).

The Torah and commandments are the end of a rope which every person can grab. If a person holds on tight, that is, he engages in Torah and *mitzvot* to please G-d and not himself, then he cleaves to G-d and merits to understand G-d's thoughts, the secrets of the Torah. The latter are the rest of the rope and are obtainable only when one cleaves to G-d completely.

We compare G-d's thoughts and the secrets of the Torah to a rope because there are many levels of imitating G-d. Consequently, there are many sections of the rope or understanding of the Torah's secrets. The degree of comprehension of the Torah's secrets is relative to the degree that one imitates G-d. There are five levels (of soul consciousness) — *nefesh, ruach, neshamah, chayah* and *yechida.* Each level has five sub-levels and five sub-sublevels such that each level is composed of at least 25 levels.

The levels are also called "worlds." Our Sages said that "in the future G-d will inherit to the righteous 310 worlds" (TB Uktzin, end). They are called worlds because the word "world" has two meanings:

(1) everyone in that world has the same feelings and sensations. Whatever one sees, hears, and feels, all in that world see, hear and feel.

(2) everyone in that world cannot conceive of anything in any other world.

We see then that there are two paradigms of comprehension:

(1) Everyone who merits a certain level knows and comprehends everything that anyone who was or will ever be at that level in previous or future generations has or will comprehend. They have common understandings as if they are in the same world. (2) Everyone at a particular level cannot know or comprehend anything on any other level, just as no one at our mundane level can know what is present in the true (Kabbalistic) world. The levels are therefore called "worlds."

For this reason, those who have attained higher levels can write books and put down their conceptions in hints and analogies. They are understood by all those who attain the level that the books pertain to. These people have a common set of comprehensions. One who has not completely attained the level of the authors will not understand the hints. And certainly those who have not at all attained the level will understand nothing for they have no comprehensions in common.

We have previously said that complete cleaving and total comprehension has 125 general levels. It is impossible to attain all 125 levels before the Messiah comes. The reason is that there are two differences between the generation of the Messiah and all others. First, one can comprehend all 125 levels only in the generation of the Messiah and in no other generation. Second, in all other generations, only a small number of people merit cleaving to G-d. As our Sages said on the sentence "I have found one in a thousand" (Eccl. 7:28), "a thousand people may enter a room,... but only one is capable of teaching" (Kohelet Rabbah, 7:38), that is of cleaving to and comprehending G-d. But in the time of the Messiah, every person will be able to cleave and to comprehend G-d. As it is written, "and the land is full of the knowledge of G-d..." (Is. 11,9), and "no longer will man tell his friend or his brother to know G-d for they will all know Me from the young to the old" (Jer. 31:34).

The exception is Rabbi Shimon Bar Yochai and his generation who wrote the Zohar. They meritted all 125 levels even before the Messiah had come. Concerning them, it is written, "a wise man is preferable over a prophet" (Zohar, Vol. I, 7b; Zohar, Vol. 2, 5b). We find it written many times in the Zohar that there will never again be a generation like that of Rabbi Shimon Bar Yoachai until the time of the Messiah. The Zohar made such a strong impact on the world because the secrets it contains include all 125 levels.

The Zohar says that it (the Zohar) will not be revealed until the end of days, that is, until the time of the Messiah. As we have stated, if the level of the reader is not the same as the author, then the reader will not understand because they don't share common comprehensions. Since the writers of the Zohar had already attained all 125 levels, it is impossible for us to understand all of it until the Messiah arrives. We conclude, therefore, that until the Messiah arrives, we don't have a common degree of comprehension with the Zohar's authors and the Zohar could not be revealed before the generation of the

Messiah.

From this we have complete proof that we have arrived at the generation when the Messiah will arrive. We know that all the explanations on the Zohar which preceeded us explained only 10 percent of the difficult passages. And in those places which were explained, the explanations are almost as difficult as the Zohar itself. In this generation, we have meritted the "Sulam" commentary, which is a complete explanation of all the Zohar. Not only this, but it does not leave a single difficult passage unexplained. Also, the explanations are based on simple logic. Every intermediate reader can understand them. The fact that the Zohar has been revealed in our generation is clear proof that we are already in the Messianic era and at the beginning of the generation wherein "the entire land is filled with knowledge of G-d" (Isaiah).

We must realize that spiritual matters are not the same as physical ones. In the physical realm, giving and receiving are simultaneous events; in spiritual matters, the two are separated. Initially, G-d gives a person the opportunity to receive, but the person has not yet received. Only when he purifies himself and makes himself holy can he receive,. In this way, much time can pass from the time G-d gives until the person receives.

Our generation has already reached the level of "the entire land shall be filled with the knowledge of G-d." This refers only to the giving aspect. We have not yet reached the point of receiving. First we must purify ourselves and study as necessary. Then we will accept what G-d has given us and the passage "the entire land shall be filled with knowledge of G-d" will be complete.

It is known that redemption and complete comprehension of

G-d are intimately tied one with the other. The proof is that anyone who is drawn to the secrets of the Torah is also drawn to the land of Israel. We are promised therefore that "the entire land..." will not be fulfilled until the end of days, that is with redemption (through the Messiah).

Until now, we have only merited being given the opportunity to attain complete comprehension. Similarly, we have not yet merited redemption but only the opportunity to be redeemed. The fact is that G-d has taken the land of Israel from the gentiles and returned it to us, but we have not yet taken it as our inheritance because the time for receiving it has not yet arrived. We do not yet have an independent economy and there can be no national independence without economic independence.

More importantly, our souls are not yet redeemed. As long as most of our citizens are still involved with their foreign cultures and are not yet prepared for, or capable of, Jewish culture, then their bodies are still prisoners of foreign powers. From this point of view, Israel is still in the hands of the gentiles. The proof is that no one is as excited by the redemption as he should be after having waited for it for 2,000 years. Few of the Jews in the Diaspora (exile) are trying to come to Israel and benefit from the redemption. Not only that, but a large portion of those who have been redeemed and now live in Israel are looking forward to returning to their countries of origin.

We see then that although G-d has taken the land of Israel from the gentiles and given it to us, we have still not received it; we still don't benefit from it. What G-d gave us is the opportunity for redemption, the chance to purify ourselves and accept upon ourselves to observe G-d's Torah and commandments. Only then will the holy temple be rebuilt and will we receive the land of Israel as our inheritance. Then we will sense and feel the joy of redemption. Until we arrive at this point, nothing has changed. There is no difference between the conduct of the land before, when the gentiles ruled it, and now. This applies to the judicial system, the economy, and the service of G-d. We have only the opportunity for redemption and not redemption itself.

The implication of what we have been saying is that our generation is the Messianic generation. This is why our holy land has been redeemed from the gentiles. We have also merited to have the Zohar revealed. That represents the start of fulfilling the Biblical prophecy that "the land shall be filled with knowledge of G-d..." (Is. 11:9) "and no man shall teach... for they shall all know me from the young to the old." (Jer. 31:34). In both these areas we have merited only that G-d gave them to us; we have not yet received anything. We have only received the opportunity to begin serving G-d, to engage in the Torah and commandments for their own sake. Then we will merit the great success that is promised for the Messianic generation. No previous generation has even known this. We can look forward to receiving two things: total comprehension and total redemption.

We have now fully explained our Sages' answer to the question of how it is possible to cleave to G-d. Their explanation that we should cleave to His qualities is correct for two reasons. First, because spiritual closeness is not measured by spatial closeness, but by equality of form. Second, because the only reason why the soul differs from G-d is that the former has a Desire to Receive. So after the Desire to Receive has been removed from the soul, the latter returns to its former state of oneness with G-d.

All of this is very theoretical. Practically speaking, they have not answered anything by saying we should cleave to His qualities. They explained that the soul must separate the Desire to Receive which is part of its nature and reverse it into a desire to impart. And the analogy we brought of a drowning man holding tightly onto the rope that is thrown to him is also incomplete. Until he permanently engages in Torah and *mitzvot* for its own sake, he is not holding on tightly to the rope.

So a question is raised again. Where will he find the motivation to work as hard as he can for G-d's satisfaction? We know that just as a motor cannot run without fuel, a person cannot make any move unless he derives some benefit from it. So if a person derives no personal benefit other than pleasing G-d, he is unmotivated to work.

The answer is that for anyone who properly understands G-d's greatness, the influence he imparts reverses and he receives from it. An example is given in the Talmud (TB Kiddushin, 7a). When an important man marries, his bride gives him money (instead of the other way around). It is considered that she received it and they are married.

The same is true of G-d. One can receive nothing more important than to properly understand G-d's greatness. This is sufficient motivation for him to work as hard as he can to do G-d's will. But if he does not properly comprehend G-d's greatness, then what he receives by imparting is not sufficient for him to worship G-d with all his heart and soul.

Whenever a person truly intends to do something solely for G-d's sake, the work involved will be minimal. But if he considers only himself then he will be like a motor without fuel, for we know that a person will not move even a single limb unless he benfits from it. And certainly he won't have the strength to devote all his heart and soul to the degree required by the Torah unless he benefits.

The truth is that to comprehend G-d's greatness to a degree where one's imparting becomes an act of receiving is not difficult. We all know that G-d created and sustains everything. We know he has no beginning and no end and that his greatness is endless. The difficulty is that greatness is something that depends not on the individual, but on the environment. For example, even if a person is filled with good qualities, if he is not respected by society then his spirit will always be weak. He will be unable to be proud of his qualities, even though he knows he possesses them. The opposite is also true. If a person with no good qualities is respected by society as if he did have them, then he will be filled with pride. Importance is seen then as a function of society.

When an individual sees how society is not serious in serving G-d and that they don't value His greatness, then he is unable to overcome society and he, too, cannot fully comprehend G-d's greatness. He acts with levity when serving G-d, just as they do. And because he lacks the foundation of comprehending G-d's greatness, then he is unable to perform for G-d's sake or for his own. He has no fuel for the task. He has no choice but to either work for himself or not work at all becasue he will not receive from G-d when serving Him.

The Bible says "the glory of a king is with a large nation" (Prv. 14:28). It applies to recognition of greatness by society in two ways: (1) the level of the society and (2) the size.

Because the task of overcoming society is so great, our Sages advised, "make for yourself a Rabbi and buy for yourself a friend" (Abot, 1:6). A person should choose for himself an important, famous person as his Rabbi. From him he can learn how to observe the Torah and *mitzvot* for the sake of giving G-d pleasure. The Rabbi eases the task in two ways. First, because he (the Rabbi) is an important person, the student can do things for his (the Rabbi's) sake. Because his Rabbi is at such a high level, then imparting to him becomes like receiving. This is a natural fuel wherewith the student can impart greatly. After he accustoms himself to impart to his Rabbi, the student can switch to engaging in Torah and *mitzvot* for G-d's sake. The habits he acquired with his Rabbi become second nature as he serves G-d.

The second way is in the help he receives from his Rabbi. When a person imitates G-d,. it is useless unless it is forever. G-d must bear witness to him that he will never revert to his old ways. This is not the case when the student imitates his Rabbi. The Rabbi is in this world for only a short time, so imitating the Rabbi is worthwhile even if the student should revert back to his old ways. Each time he imitates his Rabbi, the student temportarily cleaves to him. He understands his Rabbi's thoughts according to the degree of cleaving. The student is able to use his Rabbi's comprehension of G-d's greatness to convert his (the student's) imparting into receiving and sufficient fuel for him to dedicate his heart and soul. In this way, the student is also able to engage in Torah and *mitzvot* for G-d's sake. He does so with all his heart and soul. This is the special act which leads to everlasting cleaving to G-d.

One can now understand our Sages when they said, "serving

the Torah is greater than learning it, as it is written, here is Elisha, the son of Shafat who poured water on the hands of Elijah" (2 Kings, 3:11). It does not say learned but "poured" (TB Berakhot, 7b; Zohar, Vol. I, 98b). It is surprising how simple acts can be more important than learning wisdom and knowledge.

From what we have said, we understand that Elisha served his master (Elijah) with all his heart and soul. The service brought him to cleaving unto his master so that he received Elijah's knowledge and thoughts. This type of learning from "mouth to mouth" (active interaction) resulted in a spiritual cleaving. Through this, Elisha comprehended Elijah's greatness and all that he imparted was converted into receiving. It sufficed as fuel for Elisha to dedicate his heart and soul until he cleaved to G-d.

The same is not true for someone who only LEARNS Torah from his Rabbi. Learning is for the sake of the student and does not lead to cleaving. It can be called learning from "mouth to ear." (passive interaction). Serving his teacher leads the student to understanding of his teacher's thoughts while learning from him leads only to understanding his words. Serving the teacher compared to learning from him is like the teacher's thoughts compared to his words.

All this refers to serving his teacher for his teacher's sake. But if the service is for his own sake then it can never bring him to cleaving to his teacher. In that case, learning is far superior to service.

Above it was stated that if the society does not value the greatness of G-d, then the individual's ability to fully comprehend G-d is weakened. The same applies to a teacher. If the society does not properly recognize the teacher, this prevents the student from properly appreciating him. When our Sages said, "make for yourself a Rabbi and buy yourself a friend," (Abot, 1:), they meant that an individual can create for himself a new environment, one which will help him appreciate the greatness of his Rabbi. He should acquire friends who appreciate his Rabbi. As a result of their conversations about the greatness of the Rabbi, each one feels this greateness. In this manner, all imparting to the Rabbi is turned into receiving and fuel for the student to engage in Torah and *mitzvot* for their own sake.

The Mishnah says that the Torah is acquired in 48 stages, including the stages of serving Torah scholars and discussions with friends (Abot, 6:6). In addition to serving his Rabbi, the student needs to converse with his friends. He needs their influence to understand the greatness of his Rabbi. An individual cannot do this by himself.

There are two factors operating here. First, the student must constantly hear from society. Second, society must be large enough. As it is written, "the glory of a king is in a large nation" (Prv. 14:28).

To achieve the first situation, every student must envision himself as the smallest of all the group. He will then be able to receive from all the others. Only a lower person will be influenced by a greater person.

Every person is obligated to reach the root of his soul, this meaning that man's goal should be to cleave unto G-d. Our Sages explained that we must imitate G-d's characteristics, referring to the 10 holy *Sefirot.* Anyone who conducts himself according to them will be blessed.

We must understand why this is called cleaving to Him. Every action in the world retains an imprint of the performer. A table reflects the mind of the carpenter with all his talent, be it much or little. As he worked, he analyzed it in his mind. One who sees the finished object and thinks about what went into it joins his thoughts with those of the carpenter for the duration of his meditation.

Nothing separates spiritual entities. When they enter into physical bodies they separate physically, but their spirituality remains united. With which knife shall we cut them so they remain separated?

The major difference between spiritual entities is qualitative; they may be more or less praiseworthy. They also differ constitutionally. The mind that engages in astrology is not interested in the natural sciences. And even within each field, there are differing degrees. One may be more adept in a particular area than the other. But when two wise men are discussing a topic and they have the same degree of wisdom, then they are exactly equal.

When one person examines the works of another and fully understands how the worker's mind operated, then the two minds are united. The bond is like that when a person meets his beloved friend on the street. He hugs and kisses him and it is impossible to separate them.

Among all creatures, the potential of the human mind is the most like G-d's. It lies between G-d's and the other creatures'. Man may emit (spiritual) sparks from his mind and in so doing, its potential is returned to him.

The Bible says, "Thou has created them all in wisdom" (Ps.). G-d created everything with his wisdom. Therefore, anyone who merits to comprehend the manner and order that He created then cleaves to the intelligence that operates them and thereby cleaves to G-d.

The Torah is composed entirely of the subject of G-d's names which are relevant to our creation. When G-d was creating the world He looked into the Torah, and created accordingly. When man, using the Torah, understands G-d's mind (so to speak) then he is cleaving to G-d's mind and therefore to G-d.

Now we understand why G-d showed us His tools. Do we need them to create other worlds? No! G-d showed us His order of creation so we will know how to cleave to His characteristics and thereby to Him.

CHAPTER 10

THIS IS FOR YEHUDA — —
FROM THE COMMENTARY ON THE PASSOVER HAGGADAH

"This is the bread of affliction that our fathers ate from in the land of Egypt." (Passover *Haggadah*). The commandment of eating Matzah was given to the Israelites before they left Egypt. It was symbolic of the future redemption which would be quick. The commandment was given when they were still enslaved in anticipation of the coming redemption. This is why when we eat the matzah now we remember the time we ate it in Egypt. Now, when we are in exile, we are similarly enslaved. We also have in mind that, as a result of this *mitzvah,* the final redemption will come soon, just as it did for our forefathers. We recite, "This year we are slaves. Next year we will all be free men" (Passover *Haggadah).*

This is what we said above. When we eat the matzah, we awaken the promised redemption. (See the introduction to Tikkunei Zohar, pars. 340-343 and in the commentary of Ma'alot Hasulam).

"WE WERE SLAVES..." (PASSOVER HAGGADAH)
We learn in the Talmud (TB Pesachim, 116b) that we begin with disgrace and finish with praise. Two Rabbis, Rab and

Shmuel held different opinions on the application of this principle. Rab said that we should begin from "In the beginning our fathers were idol worshippers." Shmuel said to begin from "we were slaves." Shmuel's opinion is followed.

We must understand how they differ. The reason for beginning with disgrace and finishing with praise is to emphasize the "advantage of light over darkness" (Eccl. 2:13). We mention the disgrace in order that the loving kindness G-d showed us will be all the more apparent. In this way, we know that our origins were from the period of disgrace when G-d did not visit us with His love.

The Kabbalah says, that G-d created the world EX NIHILO, (from nothing). Everything was absent before then. But this absence is different for everything created.

We divide creation into the four categories —— inanimate, plant, animal and man. The inanimate category was created from total absence. Plant life did not originate from total absence, but from partial absence as represented by the inanimate category. This is why planting and decay are necessary factors for every seed. These properties were taken from the inanimate category.

The same is true of the animal and human categories. Plant life is considered an absence compared to animal life, and similarly animal life compared to humans. When the Bible says, "man is born a wild ass' colt" (Job, 11:12) it is teaching us that the animal stage preceeded man. Every person must have this stage as an antecedent. Elsewhere, the Bible says, "G-d will save animal and man" (Ps., 36:7). G-d makes everything that an animal needs to live available to it. Similarly, he brings to man everything that he needs to live and prosper.

What advantage does man have over an animal? The answer lies in their needs, for the needs of a man are certainly different from those of an animal. The difference in G-d's salvation is dependant on this degree of difference.

After much study and investigation, we find no specific need or desire that a man has which an animal does not also possess. The only exception is the desire to cleave to G-d. Only man is capable of doing this. The entire essence of man's creation is the natural attraction he has to serve G-d. This is the advantage he has over the animals. Many have previously spoken about this similarity. They say that many species even display logical behavior and social tendencies.

Now we can understand the absence that existed prior to the creation of man. It represents the absence of a desire to come close to G-d, as exists at the animal level. When the Mishnah says, "We begin with disgrace and finish with praise," it means that we must remember and contemplate the absence that existed prior to man's creation. This is the absence that preceeds the praise. Through understanding the absence, we have a better undersanding of the ultimate praise.

The Israelite nation has been exiled four times, each exile preceeding a redemption. The fourth redemption will be total and complete. Exile represents the absence which preceeds the redemption. The absence prepares for the events which follow it just as planting a seed prepares for the harvest.

The Hebrew word for exile *(golah)* contains all the letters in the word redemption *(ge'ulah)* except for the letter *alef.* This letter represents the prince *(aluf)* of the world. The similarity comes to teach us that the form of the absence is the negation of existence, the latter representing redemption.

The Bible says, "no longer will man tell his fellow man... for they will all know me from the youngest to the oldest" (Jer. 31:34). The form that the absence preceeding the redemption will take is the negation of knowledge of G-d. There will be a lack of the *alef,* absent in *golah* (exile) but present in *ge'ulah* (redemption). There will be no cleaving to the prince of the world, G-d. Cleaving is our redeemer, nothing more and nothing less!

In order to understand how the absence itself prepares for the things to follow it, we will take a practical example. We know that freedom is a very high principle. Only a few of the chosen experience it and then only after much preparation. Most of the population are incapable of experiencing it and fully comprehending it. From this aspect, great and little people are equal.

The Polish nation, for example, lost control of their land only because most of them did not properly value their freedom. They therefore fell under the domination of Russia for 100 years. During that time, they all sighed under the weight of their burden. Young and old prayed for freedom. They did this even though they themselves could not properly imagine what it meant to be free. But in the absence of freedom, each one naturally longed for it.

In spite of this, after they were freed from Russian domination, many of them were astonished and totally unaware of what they had just acquired with their freedom. Some were even sorry and complained that the new government made them pay taxes and serve the country more than the previous rulers. They wished that the original government had continued. Apparently, these people did not fully appreciate the absence of freedom.

Now we understand how Rab and Shmuel differed (see beginning of this chapter). Rab explained that by beginning at the time of Terach (the Father of the patriarch Abraham) we have a greater appreciation of the redemption. By the time we were in Egypt (hundreds of years later), some of the people already loved and served G-d. The added burden of slavery to the Egyptians is not a lack in and of itself.

Shmuel disagrees with Rab. He feels that the concept of a nation being free to know G-d is a very lofty one. Only a chosen few understand it properly, while most of the population do not. The concept of difficult slavery is one that everyone can grasp. The Biblical commentator Ibn Ezra says (beginning of Mishpatim), "nothing is more difficult for a person to endure than to be at the mercy of another."

Shmuel explains the Mishnah that the absence prepares for existence. It is therefore a part of the redemption and we must thank G-d for it, too. In Shmuel's opinion, we don't begin from "...our fathers worshipped idols" because that time period is not part of the absence that preceeded the Exodus. Our fathers were the total opposite of human form because they were so far from loving G-d.

We begin from the Egyptian slavery because the flames of G-dly love were already burning in their hearts. Shortness of breath and hard work had extinguished them. This was the absence which preceeded existence and we therefore begin from "we were slaves."

CHAPTER 11

UNIFICATION

When a person begins to get to know another, he recognizes first the physical appearance. As the friendship progresses, he also recognizes the friend's knowledge and his mind. Thereafter, even if his friend is gone, only the physical eyes miss him. The spiritual eyes which have cleaved to his mind do not miss him. The friend's mind is within the first person's memory just as before, unchanged. The person's mind also does not miss the shape of the friend's body.

What follows from this is that we see only the physical shape of a person and not his entire self. When we see him regularly, then once we have completely grasped his mind and thought processes, seeing him is sufficient for us to cleave to him.

We may apply this generalization to understand processes not of this (physical) world. Our goal in life is to comprehend the Doer, G-d, along with His Intelligence. We must comprehend both, as either alone is incomplete. Once we have grasped this once, then (G-d) need not constantly be perceived. His works are enough to keep Him in our minds. After all, if G-d remains with a person long enough for that person to grasp His Intelligence, it is not right that it should be without purpose.

The desire to cleave to G-d is not an intrinsic physical part of the one who cleaves, but of his intelligence. Cleaving is a spiritual to spiritual matter; physical senses and spiritual intelligence are incompatible entities. The sole purpose of the physical senses are to reveal the intelligence so that every act will reflect the intelligence that performed it.

We will expand on this issue and explain the secret of unification of G-d which the Kabbalistic books speak of. The secret depends on the quality of negation. (The meditator) negates the absence of any potential from G-d. Everything is unified withim Him.

For example, names such as wise and kind imply the qualities of wisdom and loving-kindness. (It is foolish to ask the exact nature of these qualities). Wisdom and loving-kindness can increase by natural means. This is not true of "yichud" (unification). This concept is enhanced specifically by meditation on opposite properties. It is only through the concept of its opposite that we understand the aspect of unification. It is like a shadow that extends from a person, or a slave who follows his master.

Unification is increased to the degree of meditation on its opposite. For this reason, we will examine the different systems of understanding G-d.

Those who worship G-d in other ways *(Abodah Zarah)* fall into several groups: The first group says that G-d created the world and then transcended. He left it alone and no longer observes what happens. He certainly does not need his creatures. G-d gave supervision of the world to his seconds and to the constellations. For this reason, the group worships the signs of the zodiac.

The second group says that there is no force above nature. Everything depends on either luck or a person's diligence. Laziness is detrimental and initiative is beneficial. Occasionally a person may havew a lucky day or a lucky hour.

The third group comprises the non-Jews. They say that G-d chose the Israelite nation and gave them the Torah and commandments. Since the Israelites sinned and were wicked, G-d has forever forsaken them in favor of another nation. The length of the exile is proof of this .

The fourth group recognizes their master and intend to anger Him and rebel against His laws. They say that since G-d gave us ther laws and names with which He created the heavens and earth, these names have eternal power. Even one who does not perform G-d's commandments and find favor in His eyes may draw upon His influence through angels. This is the sin of the generations of the Tower of Babel and Noah's flood. The Midrash says that the people who reprimanded Jeremiah for prophesying on the destruction of the Temple said, "I can float on water" (Midrash Eikhah Rabba, ch. 1).

Another group says that there are two G-ds; one created good and the other created evil. According to their investigations, G-d may be divided into parts. Since they see opposite actions in this world, they made separate powers for each (see chap. 4). One power is responsible for the good in the world and the other for the bad.

The Bible says, "Former of light and creator of darkness, maker of peace and creator of evil. I, G-d, did all of these" (Is. 45:7). We see explicitly that G-d directs His world and through this, the great power of His unity is made known to all creatures. He leaves room for all the above misunderstandings to exist. Their thoughts are already included within His mighty unity. As the Bible says, "And yet a little while and the wicked are no more; you shall look at his place and he is not" (ps.37:10).

IN MEMORY OF

DAVID WEISFELD

יהושע מנשה סתהון
בן לאה

נשמתו תנוח בגן עדן

לעילוי נשמת

רבקה לאה
בת אליהו ופריידל ז"ל

נפטרה בר"ח אלול תשל"ו 1976
נולדה בה' שבט   תשי"ח 1958

Joseph ben Dov & Feige

לחיים ארוכים ובריאים

אלחנן בן דינה ויוסף

הצלחה ובריאות

זהבה בת דינה ויוסף

לבריאות

מאיתן וג'ודי ובנם יהונתן